WITNESS LEE

THE
Revelation
AND
Vision
OF
God

LIVING STREAM MINISTRY

Anaheim, California • www.lsm.org

First Edition, December 2000.

ISBN 978-0-7363-1119-9

Published by

Living Stream Ministry
2431 W. La Palma Ave., Anaheim, CA 92801 U.S.A.
P. O. Box 2121, Anaheim, CA 92814 U.S.A.

Printed in the United States of America

14 15 16 17 18 / 10 9 8 7 6 5

CONTENTS

PREFACE

This book is a translation of messages given in Chinese by Brother Witness Lee at the full-time training in Taipei, Taiwan in September 1986. These messages were not reviewed by the speaker.

Chapter One

CONCERNING THE DIVINE TRINITY

(1)

Scripture Reading: Matt. 28:19; John 14:16; Gen. 1:26; Exo. 3:14-15; John 4:24

OUTLINE

I. The first point of the vision—concerning the Divine Trinity:
   A. The revelation in the Bible—the Father, the Son, and the Spirit.
   B. Theological expressions used throughout the ages:
      1. In Greek—*hupostases, prosopa, ousia.*
      2. In Latin—*personae, essentia.*
      3. In English—*hypostases,* persons, substance, essence.
      4. In Chinese—*san-wei-i-t'i.*

AN INTRODUCTORY WORD

The meaning of what we refer to as the full-time training is very broad. During the past several weeks in the training you have received many different courses. Now I will offer you yet another course, which is different from all that you received before. Therefore, you must endeavor to enter into it. In this term of the training I hope to speak specifically on "The Revelation and Vision of God." The messages, each of which is a spiritual weapon, can be used not only for this term of the training. After being compiled into a textbook, they can also be used in future trainings either in the form of videotapes or through the presentation of the co-workers. Moreover, they can be used not only in Taipei today but also abroad in the future.

THE MEANING OF *REVELATION* AND *VISION*

You are familiar with these two words: *revelation* and *vision*. However, the recently saved ones who have come into the church life for only a short time may not fully understand what *revelation* and *vision* mean. Generally, in their concept, people consider these two words synonyms, thinking that a revelation is a vision and a vision is a revelation. Actually, they are two different things.

This is what revelation means: A scene that includes all kinds of persons, things, and matters is covered, concealed, by a veil so that the mysteries contained therein cannot be known; then one day the veil is opened and the scene behind it is shown. This is revelation. The Chinese expression *ch'i shih* means "to open" and "to show." In Greek, the word for *revelation* means "the opening of the veil."

In the Bible many spiritual, divine, heavenly persons, things, and matters were hidden in God, who created all things (Eph. 3:9), and became therefore hidden mysteries. Then one day God opened the veil to us so that we were able to see the mysteries behind it. This is revelation. In the Bible there is a book called Revelation, indicating that it opens the mysteries and shows them to us. Hence, revelation is God's opening of the veil and disclosing of everything to us.

What is vision? Literally, the Chinese expression *i-hsiang* means an "uncommon, special scene." Hence, *vision* denotes an extraordinary scene. For example, someone may have a house with exquisite decorations. Once you enter in and take a look, you immediately sense something uncommon. To you that is an uncommon scene; that is a vision. In the Bible vision refers to the scenery we see from God. Through His Word God has opened the veil, but we must see the scenes contained in the Word. Whatever we see through God's revelation is a vision.

WHAT THE OLD TESTAMENT SAINTS SAW

The opening of the veil is a revelation; behind the veil is the mystery hidden in God. However, in the Bible throughout the ages the seekers of God, from Adam to John the Baptist, were only groping at the veil. We cannot say that they did not touch anything. Nevertheless, the things they touched were mostly fragmentary and incomplete; some were not quite accurate, while others were not quite thorough. For example, many words in the Psalms came out of the groping by the saints in the Old Testament. Hence, some of the things they said were correct and accurate, while other things they said were incorrect and inaccurate. This is because they were like blind men feeling an elephant, each grasping a different part and none being able to grasp the whole picture.

WHAT JOHN THE BAPTIST, PETER, PAUL, AND JOHN SAW

At the beginning of the New Testament, when John the Baptist came, it seemed that the veil was going to be opened, yet it was still not opened. In John the Baptist we still cannot see much of the mystery hidden in God. Then while the Lord Jesus was on the earth, once when He was in the region of Caesarea Philippi, He asked the disciples, "Who do men say that the Son of Man is?" They said, "Some, John the Baptist; and others, Elijah; and still others, Jeremiah or one of the prophets." This means that those people were like blind men feeling the elephant. The Lord Jesus went on and asked, "But you, who do you say that I am?" Simon Peter answered and said, "You are the Christ, the Son of the living God"

(Matt. 16:13-16). What Peter saw was wonderful, yet probably only a crack was opened between the veils for him to have a peek (v. 17). This is why afterwards he still said so many foolish things.

Another time that Peter spoke a foolish word was in Acts 10. While Peter was praying on the housetop, a trance came upon him; he saw a certain vessel like a great sheet descending from heaven, in which were all the four-footed animals, the reptiles of the earth, and the birds of heaven. Then a voice came to him, saying, "Rise up, Peter; slay and eat!" At that moment he spoke a foolish word: "By no means, Lord, for I have never eaten anything common and unclean" (vv. 9-16). The vision in the region of Caesarea Philippi is like the rising sun that has not yet appeared in full; the vision on the day of Pentecost is like the sun at noontime. Nevertheless, in Acts 10, Peter, being confused again, lost the vision. Although a vision came to him, he could not take it. He received a vision, but he could not understand it.

It was in Paul that the revelation of the mystery was greatly laid open, unveiled. But as a whole, there was still a small part that was not yet unveiled. It was not until the writing of the book of Revelation by the elderly John that the revelation of the mystery was completely laid open. Revelation means the opening of the veil. The book of Revelation completely opens the final details; that is, it opens the seven seals (5:5) which sealed up the scroll, the mystery of God, held in the right hand of the Lord Jesus. In the record of Revelation, the seven seals are opened one by one. After the opening of the seventh seal, there are the seven trumpets (8:2), which are the contents of the seventh seal. The book of Revelation first opens the veil and then blows the trumpet. To trumpet means to proclaim loudly, to make clear. It is not enough only to open the veil and break the seals; there is still the need for a loud trumpeting, a shouting. After the opening of the seventh seal, there is the blowing of the seven trumpets one after another. Furthermore, the seventh trumpet includes the seven bowls (16:1). At this time, the veil is completely opened.

THE VEIL COMPLETELY OPENED
IN THE LORD'S RECOVERY

Today to the Lord's recovery the veil has been completely opened, but to many of the clergy in Catholicism and the pastors and ministers in Protestantism it may still be closed. If you ask them, "What is the book of Revelation?" They will probably answer, "It is better not to touch it or pay attention to it; otherwise, you will get into trouble." Not only so, the Catholic Church and some of the Protestant denominations have even gone back to the Old Testament. For example, the robes that their priests wear are altogether patterned after the Old Testament. This proves that they have closed the veil again. Therefore, Catholicism is a "veiled religion," a religion without revelation. The characteristic of the Lord's recovery, however, is that the veil has been completely opened from the first chapter of Genesis to the last chapter of Revelation. If you have spent time to study the publications put out among us, especially in the last ten years, you will see that the veil has been fully opened among us. Take the latest publication, *God's New Testament Economy,* as an example. This book has a total of forty-four chapters, the last nineteen of which are on the final scene—the New Jerusalem. I can say that the New Jerusalem, not only in its contents but even in all its details, has been fully explained and completely opened to you. This is why it is included as part of your curriculum, and I fully agree with this.

THE SHALLOW AND SEALED CONDITION
OF CHRISTIANITY

A number of times people have brought me to take a tour of manufacturing plants, showing me all the interior furnishings and machinery, but I could not understand the things I saw, nor was I interested in them. While people were explaining to me, in my heart I was probably considering the significance of Exodus chapter nineteen. Since I was "absent-minded," I could not understand one bit of what I saw. Today the Bible, including the last book, Revelation, is already in our hands. In this sense the Bible should be an unveiling, a revelation, yet many professors and students of theology as

well as pastors and ministers still cannot understand the
meanings in the depths of the Bible, even though they study
it every day.

Last year when I returned here, I bought a copy of the New
Testament with Psalms and Proverbs appended. Westerners
like to add Psalms at the back of the New Testament; the
purpose of this is to teach people how to be devout as well as
to instruct them how to pray, praise, and endure sufferings.
The majority of the Chinese like maxims, and according to my
knowledge, the best maxims in the world are found in the
book of Proverbs in the Holy Bible. Therefore, the Chinese
added Psalms and Proverbs at the back of the New Testament. Three days ago, having a little leisure time, I opened
such a New Testament that I bought recently and discovered
two pictures printed at the end. One picture shows a palace, a
cobweb hanging from its wall, and a small creature crawling
on the cobweb. The Scripture cited is Proverbs 30:28, which
says, "The spider taketh hold with her hands, and is in kings'
palaces" (King James Version). A small creature crawls on a
cobweb, yet she lives in a king's palace. This is man's knowledge of the Proverbs. The other picture shows a heap of
thorns and nettles and a pile of stones; the Scripture verse
cited is Proverbs 24:31, which says, "And there it was,
all overgrown with thorns; / Its surface was covered with nettles, / And its stone wall was broken down." Why was it so
desolated? The following verses say, "When I looked, I considered it; / I saw it and received instruction: / A little sleep, a
little slumber, / A little folding of the hands to rest, / And your
poverty will come upon you like a robber, / And your want,
like an armed man" (vv. 32-34). I am very familiar with these
verses. Over sixty years ago a famous traveling preacher in
China wrote a message, entitled, "The Evil Consequences of a
Sluggard," based upon these verses. As a newly saved one,
I was deeply moved after reading that message; I felt that I
should not be lazy anymore but should work diligently
instead. I often asked myself, "Is there a heap of thorns or
nettles on the ground of my house? Is there a pile of stones
and mud? If so, clean up!" That was my condition in the first
year after I was saved. Gradually, however, when I studied

the Bible in a deeper way, I stopped paying attention to the thorns, nettles, and fallen stones. Instead, all I saw was the economy, the mystery, and the vision of God.

Dear brothers and sisters, please consider: You have the New Testament here, and you also have Psalms and Proverbs here, but at the end these two pictures are printed. What does this show? It shows that people have seen only this much. The vision they have received is that a small creature crawls on the wall and lives in the palace and that we should not be lazy but be diligent instead. Furthermore, in America some famous preachers are preaching on television, "The Secret of Success," teaching people how to open factories and manage banks by trusting in God and praying to the Lord that they may have a successful enterprise, become prosperous, and make a lot of money. The live audience consists mostly of businessmen in their thirties or forties. They are greatly encouraged and recognize that Jesus is believable and God is worthy of their worship. They believe that all they need is to worship and believe in God and their business will prosper and be successful. This is the fallen and pitiful condition of today's Christianity.

SPEAKING THE ECONOMY OF GOD
AND THE MYSTERY OF HUMAN LIFE

Today you are serving the Lord full-time, but I would like to ask you: In your full-time work for the Lord what do you preach to people? Do you tell people how restful it is that a small creature crawls on the wall yet lives in the palace? Or do you tell them that the evil consequences of the sluggard are thorns, nettles, and fallen stones? Or do you tell them the secret to a successful business? What do you preach when you go out to knock on doors? You need to preach the economy of God and the mystery of human life.

Not too long ago when I went back to Anaheim, I heard two testimonies on door-knocking in a Chinese-speaking meeting. One brother said that he testified for twenty minutes about how he escaped by swimming from the mainland China to Hong Kong. Some were moved by his testimony and expressed their desire to believe in the Lord, but no one was

baptized. Another two brothers testified that they met someone during their door-knocking. They wanted to preach the
gospel to him, but he said he had no time. The brothers said,
"It will take only a few minutes." Then they opened the booklet, *The Mystery of Human Life,* and read a paragraph with
him. They went on to tell him that God has an economy and
that man was created with three parts—spirit, soul, and
body, with the spirit being the innermost part into which God
desires to enter and dwell. In less than fifteen minutes that
person was baptized in a saint's house nearby. Brothers and
sisters, which one of the two testimonies would you imitate?
Only the blind, due to their ignorance, would appreciate the
first testimony. By this you can see that when you go into
people's homes, you should not give lengthy testimonies or
speak your own words. Moreover, you should not talk about
the small creature in the kings' palaces or about not being
lazy. You should present *The Mystery of Human Life* to people
and lead them to contact the Lord's word directly. This is the
secret of today's preaching of the gospel by door-knocking to
lead people to believe, be baptized, and be saved.

I. THE FIRST POINT OF THE VISION— CONCERNING THE DIVINE TRINITY

A. The Revelation in the Bible— the Father, the Son, and the Spirit

My burden is not to give you lessons one after another;
rather, my burden is to give you a secret so that you will have
something to apply when you go out to preach the gospel by
door-knocking. The secret is the revelation and vision of God.
Beginning with this message we will use one scene after
another to speak about the revelations of God and explain the
visions that we have seen therein. The Bible contains God's
revelations, but you need to see them. Once you see them,
they become visions.

The first scene of the revelation in the Bible is the Triune
God—the Father, the Son, and the Spirit. When Christianity
was first brought to China, the missionaries translated
their biblical knowledge and some theological doctrines into

Chinese. It was not an easy task in those early days. The Bible does not have the expression *the Triune God;* the earliest Chinese translation of the term *Trinity* was *san-wei-i-t'i,* that is, "three persons, one substance." Hence, before we speak about the revelation of the Triune God, we need to know the history of the development of Christianity in China.

The Doctrine
of "Three Persons, One Substance"
in Chinese Christian Theology

In A.D. 431 the Council of Ephesus condemned the sect of Nestorius as heretical. However, this sect gained many believers in Syria and was protected by the Persian Empire. In the seventh century, during the Tang Dynasty, Nestorianism spread into China. At the same time, it spread also to southern India and became the origin of Christianity in India. The missionaries who brought Nestorianism to China concentrated their activities mostly in the region of Sian, the capital at that time, and they preached primarily to the officials and scholars. Nestorianism was received by several emperors, and a number of temples were built. Today there is still a Nestorian tablet with an inscription that contains the phrase *ch'ing feng,* which literally means "clear breeze," denoting the Holy Spirit. This implies that Nestorianism did not have much knowledge of the truth. Later, the flourishing of Buddhism influenced some of the emperors who prohibited the activities of Nestorianism and destroyed its temples. Eventually, due to its lack in truth and life, Nestorianism vanished.

In the sixteenth century during the Ming Dynasty, Catholicism spread to China. The Catholics rendered *the Holy Spirit* as *the Holy God* and rendered *God* as *the Lord of Heaven;* this brought in some difficulties in translation. Later, the Western missionaries went to the Orient. Generally, the translations put out by the various denominations were about the same, and even some of the expressions were the same as those used in Catholicism. It was then that the term *Trinity* was translated into Chinese as *san-wei-i-t'i,* which literally means "three persons, one body (substance)." I was born, educated, and reared in Christianity, and I also memorized the doctrine of *san-wei-i-t'i*. Yet I did not understand what it was all about, nor did I know whether the word *t'i* refers to a group of people as a corporate body, to the physical body, or to a body with a shape. In 1958 while I was traveling in Greece, I saw a painting in an Eastern Orthodox Church of a man with a body and three heads who looks like a monster. When I saw that, I felt that it corresponds with the phrase "three persons, one body" that I read in my youth.

Until this day I still do not fully understand what the phrase "three persons, one body" refers to in Chinese theology. The most important statement in Chinese theology about the Trinity is that there should be "neither the confounding of persons nor the dividing of the body (substance)." The "persons" are the three Persons in the Godhead—the Father, the Son, and the Spirit. That there should be no confounding of persons means that the Father is the Father, the Son is the Son, and the Spirit is the Spirit; there should be no confounding of the three. Furthermore, the "body (substance)" is one and cannot be divided. This is the primary significance of the doctrine of the Trinity in Chinese theology.

The Study concerning the Triune God in Theology throughout the Ages

Now we will go on to see the study concerning the Triune God throughout the ages. The New Testament is divided mainly into three sections: the Gospels and the Acts, the Epistles, and Revelation. The Gospels primarily recorded the ministry and revelation of the Lord Jesus. Then the apostles wrote the Epistles as a continuation of the revelation of the Lord Jesus; the most important writer among them was Paul. Lastly, the apostle John wrote Revelation. After the writing of Revelation was finished, the Lord's word clearly indicates that the revelation of God has been completed and that no one should add anything to it, nor should anyone take away anything from it (22:18-19). Theologians and godly people throughout the generations have acknowledged that after the apostle John finished writing Revelation, the revelation of God has been completed and nothing more can be added.

After the passing away of the apostles, there were the so-called church fathers in church history. Raised up at the end of the first century and in the middle of the second century, they were a group of people, including both Jews and Gentiles, who expounded the biblical truths. They studied extensively the writings of the apostles as well as the contents of the Old Testament and had high theological attainments. Due to their research, the term *Trinity* was coined. Although the Bible does not have the term *Trinity,* it has the Trinity as a fact.

The studies and records of the church fathers were all in Greek. In the sixth century, around A.D. 570, the papal system was officially instituted and widely recognized by the churches; thus, a catholic church was formed, which became the antecedent of the Roman Catholic Church. From around A.D. 100 to the formation of the papal system at the end of the sixth century, this period of four to five hundred years was called "The Period of Councils" in church history. Theological studies during this period continued to be written in Greek.

After the establishment of the Catholic Church with its headquarters in the city of Rome, where Latin was used most prevailingly, theological studies entered the second stage, the stage of the Latin language. From the seventh century to the sixteenth century, theological literature was written chiefly in Latin. Even during the Reformation, Martin Luther still used Latin in his writings, although he was German. Therefore, Latin also occupies quite an important position in theological research.

Then in the 1700s, during the time of Zinzendorf and John Wesley, theological studies gradually turned from Latin to English. In particular, in the beginning of the nineteenth century when the Brethren were raised up, their opening up of the Bible had a tremendous influence on the teaching of biblical truths. Even to the present time, the essential, fundamental theology in Protestantism, both in Europe and America, is still ninety percent based upon the Brethren theology. Then the spread of theology to China produced the Chinese theology. The language in Chinese theology evolved from Greek,

Latin, and English. In Latin, the word *triune* is used for the Trinity. *Tri* means "three" and *une* means "one"; hence, *triune* means "three-one," being both three and one. This is why fifty years ago, based upon this, we changed the expression *three persons, one body* in Chinese theology into the expression *three-in-one,* which we used for many years. Then we felt that even adding the word *in* is misleading, so we dropped it; now we simply say "the three-one God," that is, "the Triune God." According to the pure revelation of the Bible, God is triune; He is the Triune God.

B. Theological Expressions Used throughout the Ages

1. Concerning the Development of the Theology of the Trinity in the Greek Language— Hupostases, Prosopa, Ousia

Why does the Triune God have the aspect of being three? To answer this question we have to study from the theology in the Greek language to the theology in the Latin language. In Greek theology, concerning the study of the Trinity, regardless how hard they tried, the theologians were not able to find any suitable expression from the Holy Scriptures; eventually they found the word *hupostasis* (singular). *Hupo* means "underneath" and *stasis* means "a supporting substance"; *hupostasis,* therefore, means "a supporting substance erected underneath." For example, the three legs of a three-legged table are the *hupostases* (plural) of the table. In Paul's Epistles this word is rendered as *confidence* or *assurance* (cf. 2 Cor. 9:4; Heb. 3:14), referring to something on which one can stand firmly. This means that the Triune God has three *hupostases,* three substantial, dependable supports—the Father, the Son, and the Spirit. These three—the Father, the Son, and the Spirit—are the three supports of the Triune God.

Concerning the aspect of the Divine Trinity's being three, another Greek word that is used is *prosopa,* which is equivalent to the Latin word, *personae,* from which the English word *person* is derived. However, most people today are not clear about the meanings of these terms. This is why Philip Schaff, a church historian, was in favor of using the Greek word *hupostases,* supporting substances, instead of the other terms.

Hupostases refers to the aspect of the Divine Trinity's being three. Nevertheless, the Divine Trinity is one in His essence. The Greek word for essence is *ousia,* denoting the essence of the substance. In Latin it is *essentia,* equivalent to the English word *essence.* The Triune God has three *hupostases* but only one *ousia.* In other words, to explain this according to the Chinese theology, we may say that the Triune God has three persons but only one essence; the persons should not be confounded and the essence should not be divided; the Father, the Son, and the Spirit are three in person, but They are one in essence.

2. Concerning the Development of the Theology of the Trinity in the Latin Language— Personae, Essentia

When the theological studies entered into the Latin language, the term *personae* was used to refer to the aspect of the Divine Trinity's being three. This word has three meanings: first, it was used in the ancient Roman Empire to refer to the masks put on by an actor in playing different roles; second, it refers to a role in a play, and by extension, to the role of one with an important position in a government or to the role of a significant member of a family; and third, it denotes "person." With regard to the aspect of the Divine Trinity's being one, the word *essentia* in Latin is used; it denotes "essence," "intrinsic nature."

3. Concerning the Development of the Theology of the Trinity in the English Language— Hypostases, Persons, Substance, Essence

Hypostases, which is the Greek word *hupostases* anglicized, means "substantial, dependable supports"; *stasis* is equivalent to the English word *substance,* referring to something real and substantial. Out of the Latin word *personae* came the word *persons,* and the Greek word *ousia* became the word *essence.*

4. Concerning San-wei-i-t'i in the Chinese Language

When the Western missionaries came to China, they used a simple expression, *san-wei-i-t'i,* to express the concept of the Divine Trinity. *Wei* denotes "person," "substance"; *t'i* refers neither to a physical body nor to a corporate body, but to an entity, to the essence of a substance. Therefore, *san-wei-i-t'i* means that although the Father, the Son, and the Spirit are three in person or in substance, They are one in essence.

FIGHTING THE GOOD FIGHT FOR THE TRUTH

Fifteen years ago in Hong Kong I released some messages on the person of Christ. These messages were later compiled into a book entitled, *Concerning the Person of Christ.* This book clearly outlines six heresies throughout the ages and one proper explanation concerning the person of Christ. This is altogether based upon the research done by the theologians in the past. Recently, a publication was put out in Hong Kong that covers exactly the same things in the same sequence. I would like to speak a word to all of you who are learning to serve the Lord: The way of the Lord's recovery today is a way that completely repudiates the traditions of Christianity, including Catholicism. Of course, those who are in Christianity are not happy with us since we renounce what they teach. Formerly, in mainland China Brother Watchman Nee was the target of the attacks from Christianity. Afterward, when I was sent abroad, I also became a target, even though that was not what I wanted to be. In America because of our proclaiming the truth, we were libeled and slandered and were therefore forced to file two lawsuits. In one case there was a settlement, and the opposing party issued a public apology in the newspapers. In the other case the opposing party, after losing, intentionally declared bankruptcy. By presenting the truth, we have quelled the waves; now there is no more scornful reviling. However, in the East the situation is still unclear. In the future wherever you go, whether in the East or in the

West, you will meet people who are in Christianity. The most important thing is that you should be able to present the truth concerning the Triune God. Therefore, I feel that I should help you to have a clear knowledge to understand the pure revelation of the Holy Scriptures.

THE PURE REVELATION OF THE BIBLE CONCERNING THE TRIUNE GOD

We all acknowledge that the matter of God's being triune is a mystery, and it is also a difficult subject. In order to speak it accurately, we must study the Scriptures in a deep and thorough way. The degree of thoroughness you have in knowing the Scriptures determines the degree of your accurateness. In studying this matter, we have stood on the shoulders of our predecessors, but we also have seen something further. Therefore, our study is more advanced, thorough, and accurate.

To know the Triune God, first we must understand the word *hupostases,* which refers to the three substances of the Divine Trinity. These three substances are the Father, the Son, and the Spirit. In the entire Bible, Matthew 28:19 is the only verse that clearly puts the Father, the Son, and the Spirit together. As the incarnated God, the Lord Jesus lived a human life on the earth, died on the cross, and resurrected after three days; then in resurrection He came to His disciples and said, "Go therefore and disciple all the nations, baptizing them into the name of the Father and of the Son and of the Holy Spirit." Although the Father, the Son, and the Spirit are three, the word *name* in Greek is singular. This means that the Father, the Son, and the Spirit are three substantially, yet They are one essentially.

We dare not say that the Father, the Son, and the Spirit are three persons, nor do we dare say that They are not, because this is truly a mystery. In John 14:16 the Father, the Son, and the Spirit all have Their respective pronouns. This verse says, "And I will ask the Father, and He will give you another Comforter, that He may be with you forever." The three pronouns *I, He,* and *He* refer to the Son, the Father, and the Spirit respectively. Now we have to go back and look at Genesis 1:26. There it tells us that in creating man, God said,

"Let Us make man in Our image, according to Our likeness." The pronouns used in this verse are plural: *Us* and *Our*. To say, based upon these pronouns, that there are three Gods becomes another extreme, which is also a heresy, since both the Old Testament and the New Testament strongly reiterate that there is only one God. Isaiah 45:5 says, "I am Jehovah and there is no one else; / Besides Me there is no God." Also, 1 Corinthians 8:4 says, "There is no God but one."

Moreover, Exodus 3:14-15 says, "And God said to Moses, I AM WHO I AM...Jehovah, the God of your fathers, the God of Abraham, the God of Isaac, and the God of Jacob....This is My name." Here, *Jehovah* denotes the Triune God. God is Jehovah; this name also means the One "who is and who was and who is coming" (Rev. 1:4), implying three periods of time. Yet, in Exodus 3:14-15 the pronoun used is not the plural *We* but the singular *I*. Therefore, we cannot say that there are three Gods; rather, we should say that God is triune. Not only so, "the God of Abraham, the God of Isaac, and the God of Jacob" also implies that God is triune, that God has the aspect of being three.

The most important thing about the Triune God's being one is that God is one in His essence. John 4:24 says, "God is Spirit, and those who worship Him must worship in spirit and truthfulness." *God* here is the complete Triune God—the Father, the Son, and the Spirit; *Spirit* in this verse refers to the divine essence. This is just like saying that wood is the nature, the essence, of a table. Therefore, if we want to worship God, who is Spirit, we must worship Him with our spirit, which has the same nature as His.

THE NECESSITY OF BEING EQUIPPED
WITH THE TRUTH

The foregoing fellowship only gives you some knowledge as a foundation. Although I cannot speak in detail, I hope that you will try your best to remember the various expressions used in the theological studies concerning the Trinity throughout the ages. Then, when you go to speak to others, you will have a solid foundation. During our lawsuit in America, whenever the opposing party came to depose me, I always presented the truth in a clear way; eventually, they had to concede defeat. The situation in today's Christianity is confusing and full of all kinds of mixtures, such as Mormonism and Jehovah's Witnesses. As you begin to learn to serve the Lord and touch His work, you must have a clear idea of some of the contents of Christianity and a thorough study of the pure truth. Only then will you be able to present the truth clearly and answer questions properly when you preach to people.

After the training in Anaheim last summer, while I was resting on a nearby mountain, I met someone who belongs to the Jehovah's Witnesses. Although he has a regular job, he is a zealous believer; he received a two-week training by the Jehovah's Witnesses and studied six thousand Scripture verses. When I saw him, I asked, "Among your people, do you recognize that Jesus is God?" He told me, "Jesus is not the eternal God; He is another kind of God." Therefore, I showed him Romans 9:5: "Christ, who is God over all, blessed forever." Eventually, he conceded defeat, but he brought another person who produced a copy of their book and said, "Yes, Romans 9:5 says that Jesus Christ is God, but this is different from the eternal God." I did not want to waste my time to continue the debate with them, since it is obvious that there cannot be two eternal Gods.

Today, in a sense, Christianity has spread to the whole earth. Wherever you go, you will meet some missionaries and encounter some obstacles. Therefore, you must understand the truth that you may be able to help and preserve the lambs who are under your leading. Otherwise, you will have brought people to salvation, but eventually when they are blown by any wind of teaching, they will begin to doubt and be carried away by the wind. For this reason, you must be equipped in the truth so that when the need arises, not only you yourself can stand and not be carried away by any wind of teaching, but you can also protect those who are under your leading by defending and confirming on their behalf.

I am not proud; I am just presenting the facts. I challenged Christianity over twenty years ago. Until today, however, no one among them has been able to refute me. This is because the truth is the truth. Now I have passed on to you a summary of the crucial points of the truths, and I hope that you will continue to propagate what you have received. As those who serve the Lord, you must be clear about the basic truths. Ephesians 6:14 says that we should gird our loins with truth and not be loose that we may protect ourselves and preserve others as well. Therefore, I have briefly put before you the crystallization of my studies for many decades, hoping that you will be established, equipped, and perfected.

CONCERNING THE DIVINE TRINITY

(2)

Scripture Reading: Gen. 1:1-2, 26; Matt. 3:16-17; John 14:9-10; 2 Cor. 3:17; John 8:16; Matt. 27:46

OUTLINE

C. Four crucial points concerning the Divine Trinity:
  1. The coexistence of the three:
     a. In the record of the Old Testament, the Father, the Son, and the Spirit being coexistent.
     b. In the record of the four Gospels, the Father, the Son, and the Spirit being coexistent.
     c. In the record of the Epistles, the Father, the Son, and the Spirit being coexistent.
     d. The three—the Father, the Son, and the Spirit—being eternal.
  2. The coinherence of the three.
  3. The essential Trinity:
     a. The Holy Spirit as the essence of the conception of the Lord Jesus.
     b. The Son coming from and with the Father, and the Father being always with the Son.
     c. The Father being with the Son in the Son's crucifixion.
  4. The economical Trinity.

C. Four Crucial Points
concerning the Divine Trinity

Concerning the Divine Trinity, we have seen the revelation of the Father, the Son, and the Spirit in the Scriptures and the theological terms used throughout the ages. In this chapter we will go on to cover four crucial points concerning the Divine Trinity: the coexistence of the three, the coinherence of the three, the essential Trinity, and the economical Trinity.

1. The Coexistence of the Three

Concerning the Divine Trinity, first of all, we must pay attention to the fact that the three of the Divine Trinity—the Father, the Son, and the Spirit—are coexistent. In theological history there was a group of people called modalists who advocated that the Father, the Son, and the Spirit were three modes of the unique God in the carrying out of redemption and that afterwards, fulfilling Their respective missions consecutively, They returned in succession to Their original unity. In other words, the modalists believed that the Father, the Son, and the Spirit were one God, yet the manifestation of this one God was divided into three periods. In the Old Testament He decreed the law and manifested Himself as the Father; that was the period of the Father in which there was only the Father without the Son or the Spirit. Then in His incarnation He manifested Himself as the Son; that was the period of the Son, and the Father was over. Finally, in the inspiring of the apostles He manifested Himself as the Holy Spirit; that was the period of the Spirit, and the Son was over. In this teaching, it is the one and the same God who appeared in successive and temporary manifestations. Of course, the teaching of modalism is a great heresy. In America some mistakenly thought that we teach modalism and therefore condemned us as modalists. The fact is that we also condemn modalism.

Most readers of the Bible, including some who are among us, think that in the Old Testament the emphasis is on the work of God the Father; that in the four Gospels the emphasis is on the work of God the Son, the Lord Jesus; and that from

Acts to Revelation the emphasis is on the work of God the Spirit, that is, the work of the Holy Spirit. We cannot say this is wrong because this is indeed what the record of the Bible shows. You can say that the period covered by the Old Testament is the period of the Father, the period covered by the four Gospels, which was a short period of a little over thirty years, is the period of the Son, and the period from the day of Pentecost to the Lord's second coming is the period of the Spirit. However, unlike what modalism teaches, this is not to say that the Father existed only until the coming of the Son and that the Son existed only until the coming of the Spirit. The Bible strongly indicates that the Father, the Son, and the Spirit are always coexistent.

a. In the Record of the Old Testament, the Father, the Son, and the Spirit Being Coexistent

Genesis 1:1 says, "In the beginning God created the heavens and the earth." Immediately after this, the latter half of verse 2 says that "the Spirit of God was brooding upon the surface of the waters." This clearly shows us that God was there and the Spirit also was there. Then in verse 26, in the creation of man, God said, "Let Us make man in Our image, according to Our likeness." The pronouns used here are *Us* and *Our*. By this we can see that it is not that only the Father was there and that the Son and the Spirit were not. Rather, the three—the Father, the Son, and the Spirit— existed there at the same time; this is why They used *Us* and *Our* to refer to Themselves.

Not only so, the Old Testament frequently says that the Spirit of Jehovah clothed someone or came upon someone (Judg. 6:34; 11:29); it also speaks about the operation, the work, of the Spirit of God (Gen. 1:2; 6:3; Job 33:4; Dan. 5:14). This shows us that the Spirit was always there in the Old Testament.

Furthermore, although the designations or names *Christ, Jesus,* and *Jesus Christ* are not mentioned in the Old Testament, a special title referring to the Lord Jesus is used, which is *the Angel of Jehovah*. In Exodus 3:2-20, three designations—*the Angel of Jehovah, Jehovah,* and *God*—are used interchangeably. This proves that the Angel of Jehovah is Jehovah and that Jehovah is God. Exodus 14:19 says that while Pharaoh and his chariots and horsemen were pursuing the children of Israel, "the Angel of God, who went before the camp of Israel, moved and went behind them." This Angel of God is the Angel of Jehovah mentioned in chapter three. Exodus 23:20-21 says, "I am now sending an Angel before you...to bring you into the place which I have prepared....For My name is in Him." The Angel mentioned in all these passages refers to the Lord Jesus. Then in Judges 13:15-21, the Angel of Jehovah appeared again. He was there speaking to Manoah. At the end Manoah asked what His name was, and He replied, "Why do you ask about My name, since it is wonderful?" This Angel of Jehovah is the Lord Jesus.

Hence, from the Old Testament we see that God is God the Father, the Angel of Jehovah is God the Son, and the Spirit of Jehovah or the Spirit of God is God the Spirit. The three— the Father, the Son, and the Spirit—existed at the same time in the Old Testament.

b. In the Record of the Four Gospels, the Father, the Son, and the Spirit Being Coexistent

Although the Gospels are concerned mainly with the Lord Jesus and take Him as the center and the subject, in these books the Father, the Son, and the Spirit still coexisted. The clearest picture is seen in the baptism of the Lord Jesus. When He came out of the water, the Father spoke to Him from the heavens while the Spirit descended upon Him like a dove (Matt. 3:16-17). In this situation, the One who spoke from the heavens was the Father; the One who descended like a dove was the Spirit; and the Lord Jesus, who stood in the water, was the Son. This picture clearly shows us that in the incarnation, the Father, the Son, and the Spirit existed at the same time. This also proves that the teaching which says that when the Son came, the Father was over, when the Son was there, the Spirit was not there, and when the Spirit came, the Son was over, is altogether without any basis and is therefore a great heresy.

c. In the Record of the Epistles, the Father, the Son, and the Spirit Being Coexistent

Then in the Epistles, from Acts to Revelation, many times the Father, the Son, and the Spirit are mentioned at the same time. For example, 2 Corinthians 13:14 says, "The grace of the Lord Jesus Christ and the love of God and the fellowship of the Holy Spirit be with you all." All three—the Father, the Son, and the Spirit—are here. Every chapter of Ephesians shows us the fact of the coexistence of the Father, the Son, and the Spirit. The most obvious passage is 3:14-17, which says, "I bow my knees unto the Father,...that He would grant you,...to be strengthened with power through His Spirit into the inner man, that Christ may make His home in your hearts through faith." Here, Paul bowed his knees to the Father that He would grant the believers to be strengthened with power through His Spirit into their inner man, that the Son, Christ, may make His home in their hearts. The Father is here, the Spirit is here, and Christ is here; the three are coexistent. Then in the last book, Revelation, the opening word in the first chapter says, "Him who is and who was and who is coming, and from the seven Spirits who are before His throne, and from Jesus Christ, the faithful Witness, the First-born of the dead, and the Ruler of the kings of the earth" (vv. 4-5). The One who was, who is, and who is coming is the Father; the seven Spirits before the throne of the Father are the Spirit; and Jesus Christ is the Son. Therefore, the three—the Father, the Son, and the Spirit—are mentioned at the same time; this proves that They are coexistent.

Hence, from the Old Testament to the Gospels, the Epistles, and Revelation there is a strong revelation that the three—the Father, the Son, and the Spirit—exist at the same time.

d. The Three—the Father, the Son, and the Spirit—Being Eternal

The three of the Divine Trinity—the Father, the Son, and

the Spirit—exist at the same time; and Their coexistence is from eternity to eternity, being equally without beginning and without ending. The Father is eternal; this can be proven by Isaiah 9:6, which refers to the Father as the "Eternal Father." The Son is also eternal. Concerning the Son, Hebrews 1:12 says, "You are the same, and Your years will not fail"; Hebrews 7:3 also says that He had "neither beginning of days nor end of life," indicating that He is eternal. Moreover, the Spirit is eternal; Hebrews 9:14 mentions "the eternal Spirit." Hence, the three—the Father, the Son, and the Spirit—all are eternal.

Concerning this point, we must know that in church history there existed another heretical sect, the Arians. To be eternal means to be without beginning or ending, to be complete and perfect, and to be infinite and boundless. Yet the Arians maintained that although Christ is the Son of God, He was not God in eternity but became God at a certain time. The Jehovah's Witnesses belong to this sect, which originated with Arius of the fourth century. Based upon Colossians 1:15b, which says, "Who [the Son of the Father's love] is...the Firstborn of all creation," Arius advocated that since Christ is a creature, He does not have the same essence (Gk. *ousia*) of God, and that although the universe and all things were created through Him (Heb. 1:2; John 1:3), His existence is not eternal but had a beginning. Therefore, Arius taught that since Christ is a creature, He cannot be equal with the Father. In other words, Arius asserted that although the Son was in eternity, He was not there in the beginning; rather, He was created by God at a certain point in eternity to be the Firstborn of all creation. This kind of teaching is a great heresy.

It is true that we believe the Son is the Firstborn of all creation, but our belief is not according to the teaching of Arius but according to the pure revelation of the Bible. The Bible says that Christ is the Firstborn of all creation not according to His divinity but according to His humanity. According to His divinity, He is the eternal God, the Creator; however, since He became flesh and put on a body of flesh and blood, He also possesses humanity. Hence, in the aspect of His being a man, He has humanity and is a creature.

In the Council of Nicaea, convened in A.D. 325, Arianism was condemned as a heresy. This is why up to the present almost no one dares to teach that Christ is a creature. Nevertheless, in church history, still there were some who properly taught that Christ is both the Creator and the Firstborn of all creation. Such ones include Robert Govett and his student D. M. Panton in the beginning of the twentieth century; based upon Colossians 1:15b, they clearly said that Christ is the Firstborn of all creation. This is according to the revelation of the Scriptures. If you do not believe this, you fall into the heresy of the Docetists, referred to in 1 John 4, who did not believe that Christ came in the flesh (vv. 1-3). The Docetists advocated that Jesus was not a real man but simply appeared to be; to them He was merely a phantasm. They asserted that the body of the Lord Jesus was not a real body but was merely a phantom. This is altogether a heresy; such a heresy undermines not only the incarnation of the Lord Jesus but also His redemption and resurrection.

We firmly believe that the Lord Jesus became a creature through incarnation. Perhaps some would say that since the Lord Jesus was incarnated two thousand years ago and Adam was created six thousand years ago, and since there were other created beings before Adam, the Lord Jesus could not have been the Firstborn of all creation. Genesis 1:1 says, "In the beginning God created the heavens and the earth." Bible readers acknowledge that *heavens* and *earth* here do not merely refer to the heavens and the earth per se, but they refer to all the heavenly things and all the things on the earth, all the things that belong to the realms of the heavens and the earth, included among which are the angels, the living things on the earth, and even Satan, since he was the top archangel before the fall (cf. Ezek. 28:13-15). According to man's view, Satan may be considered the first of the creation, because in the Bible he is addressed as "Daystar, son of the dawn" (Isa. 14:12), indicating that he was created at the beginning of the creation of the universe. But this is not God's view. According to God's eternal view, Christ is the Firstborn of all creation.

I have the basis to say this. Revelation 13:8 says that

Christ is "the Lamb who was slain from the foundation of the world." Concerning the crucifixion of Christ, however, the prophecy in Daniel 9:25-27 clearly says, "From the issuing of the decree to restore and rebuild Jerusalem until the time of Messiah the Prince will be seven weeks and sixty-two weeks....And after the sixty-two weeks Messiah will be cut off." The Messiah, referring to the Lord Jesus, was cut off at the fullness of the sixty-ninth week of the seventy weeks. History tells us that the issuing of the decree to restore and rebuild Jerusalem occurred in the twentieth year of Arta-xerxes the king (Neh. 1:1; 2:1-8). After seven weeks and sixty-two weeks, that is, four hundred eighty-three years, that was exactly the year of the crucifixion of the Lord Jesus. Thus, according to man's viewpoint, Christ was crucified less than two thousand years ago; how then could Revelation say that Christ was slain from the foundation of the world? This is God's view. According to this principle, we can understand that in eternity past the three of the Godhead held a council, in which it was decided that the second—the Son—of the Divine Trinity would come to be incarnated as a creature. From that time on, in God's eternal view, God the Son had become a creature, even the Firstborn of all creation.

Not only the Triune God as a mystery is difficult to understand and impossible to comprehend, but even incarnation is a mystery that is hard for people to understand. According to man's view, the Lord Jesus did not become flesh until two thousand years ago. Yet Genesis 18 says that when Jehovah came with two angels to visit Abraham, He had a physical body. Abraham brought water to wash His feet and prepared a rich meal for Him. Nearly all orthodox Bible scholars acknowledge that the Jehovah there is the Christ in the New Testament (John 8:56-58). As early as the time of Abraham, Christ had already appeared in a bodily form. This is truly difficult to explain or comprehend. However, according to God's view, the Firstborn of all creation is Christ. This is why He also became the instrument, the means, through which all creation came into being (John 1:3; Col. 1:16).

In summary, the three—the Father, the Son, and the Spirit—all are from eternity to eternity, being equally eternal, without beginning and without ending, and existing at the same time.

2. The Coinherence of the Three

The three—the Father, the Son, and the Spirit—not only coexist but also coinhere. The term *coinhere* applied to the Triune God means that the three—the Father, the Son, and the Spirit—exist within one another.

First of all, this is based upon the word spoken by the Lord Jesus in the Gospels. In John 14:7-10 the Lord said to the disciples, "If you had known Me, you would have known My Father also; and henceforth you know Him and have seen Him." Then Philip requested, saying, "Lord, show us the Father and it is sufficient for us." The Lord answered him, "Have I been so long a time with you, and you have not known Me, Philip? He who has seen Me has seen the Father; how is it that you say, Show us the Father? Do you not believe that I am in the Father and the Father is in Me?" We simply cannot understand the Lord's answer. How can one person be in another person and the other person also be in the one person? Let me illustrate. We often say that the husband and wife are one; this is correct. However, we cannot say that the husband is in the wife and that the wife is in the husband. Yet the oneness of the Son and the Father (10:30) is that the Son is in the Father and the Father is in the Son. This is truly beyond the comprehension of our human mind.

Besides John 14:10, the same utterance can be found in 14:20; 10:38; and 17:21, 23. These five verses all refer to the fact that the Son and the Father exist within one another at the same time. These verses are crucial to our understanding of the mystery of the Divine Trinity's being three and also one. However, these verses mention only the Father and the Son; the matter concerning the Spirit is even more profound. We can say in a general way that the three—the Father, the Son, and the Spirit—are coinherent, but the relationship between the Father and the Son is different from the relationship between the Son and the Spirit. The relationship between the Father and the Son is that the Son is in the Father and the Father is in the Son. However, we cannot find

one verse in the entire Bible that says the Spirit is in the
Son or the Son is in the Spirit. What the Bible says is that
the Son became the Spirit. Hence, 1 Corinthians 15:45b says,
"The last Adam became a life-giving Spirit"; moreover,
2 Corinthians 3:17 says that "the Lord is the Spirit."

Today among Christians there exists an erroneous traditional saying that Christ is in the Holy Spirit, that is, that the
Son is in the Spirit. We must be careful; otherwise, we will
make the same mistake. For example, the last two lines of
the second stanza of *Hymns,* #501 says, "In flesh Thou hast
redemption wrought; / As Spirit, oneness with me sought."
The line cannot be written as: "In flesh Thou hast redemption
wrought; / In Spirit, oneness with me sought." We must discern the difference between the two. I do not mean to say that
it is definitely wrong to say that "the Son is in the Spirit."
Such a statement, however, is certainly not in the Bible. What
the Bible says is that "the last Adam became a life-giving
Spirit" and that "the Lord is the Spirit." Bible expositors are
puzzled about the matter of the Son's being the Spirit. Many
of them do not dare to say that Christ is the Spirit. To avoid
being troubled or condemned, they have coined the term "the
pneumatic Christ." Nevertheless, is not the pneumatic Christ
simply the Spirit?

The work we do for the Lord is to transmit Christ to others
for their enjoyment. However, they must know who Christ is
before they can enjoy Him. Therefore, when we speak about
the enjoyment of Christ, we must tell people who Christ is; we
must also tell them clearly the way to enjoy Christ. This
involves the Divine Trinity. In brief, we can say that the
Father and the Son are one because the Lord Jesus said, "I
and the Father are one" (John 10:30). However, although the
Father and the Son are one, between Them there is still a distinction of *I* and *the Father.* We must not disregard this point,
because if we do, we would become modalists. Modalism advocates that God, who is one, has three manifestations in three
different periods and that the three manifestations do not
exist within each other at the same time. The Scriptures show
us, however, that the three—the Father, the Son, and the
Spirit—not only exist at the same time but also exist in one

another. Therefore, the three—the Father, the Son, and the Spirit—are one; They are one God. However, this one God is also three; He is the Father, the Son, and the Spirit.

Since this is the case, when are the Father, the Son, and the Spirit one, and when are They three? Bible students throughout the centuries have done a great deal of research on this point; we also have expended much effort in studying this matter. Nevertheless, no one has been able to determine when the Father, the Son, and the Spirit are three, when They are one, and when They are both three and one. According to what the Bible tells us, we can say only that God is one, yet He has the aspect of being three—the Father, the Son, and the Spirit. These three are distinct but inseparable. Furthermore, these three exist within one another: the first is in the second and the second is in the first, and the second, the Son, and the third, the Spirit, are one and the same (2 Cor. 3:17). Hence, if the Father, the Son, and the Spirit only exist at the same time, They may still be separated; however, because They also exist within one another, They are inseparable. This is why God is triune; He is the Triune God.

Brothers and sisters, by presenting these matters before you, I hope that you will be able to understand the intricacies of the Trinity. You must know and be clear about these main points. Continuing what the saints saw in the previous centuries, we have seen this much so far. The Divine Trinity is a mystery in the universe; this mystery is not for us to engage in theological debates but for us to enjoy in our practical experience.

3. The Essential Trinity

The third crucial point concerning the Divine Trinity is the essential Trinity. The Divine Trinity is absolutely one in His element and existence; His essence is absolute. Essence denotes nature; this is with respect to the Divine Trinity Himself. Today, there is a group of Christians who do not see that the Divine Trinity has the essential aspect and the economical aspect. They confuse these two aspects and therefore bring about disputes. Because I have been stressing in America that the Triune God is one and that the Father, the

Son, and the Spirit are one, they interpreted my teaching out
of context and thus condemned me for advocating modalism
like Sabellius. They said that when the Lord Jesus was
standing in the water after His baptism, the Father spoke
from the heavens while the Spirit was soaring in the air like a
dove; at that time, all three—the Father, the Son, and the
Spirit—were present but They were in three different places.
Hence, they concluded that the three of the Divine Trinity are
not only distinct but also separate. Thus, they questioned our
saying that the three are one. When I heard this kind of word
in my youth, I thought it was quite reasonable. However, I
found out gradually from my study of the Bible that in a certain aspect this reasoning is right, but it is not right in every
aspect. Actually, as far as essence is concerned, there is nothing wrong with our teaching.

a. The Holy Spirit as the Essence of the Conception of the Lord Jesus

The Gospel of Matthew not only has chapter three but also
has chapter twenty-eight. It is true that Matthew 3 has a picture showing that after His baptism the Lord Jesus was on
the earth, the Father was in the heavens, and the Spirit was
in the sky. However, the Gospel of Matthew tells us from the
beginning that God was first begotten into Mary through
the conception of the Holy Spirit and then born as Jesus
(1:18, 20-21). From that time on, you can say that Jesus was
born of the Spirit; you can also say that He was born of the
virgin Mary. This is because this wonderful One is a God-man,
possessing both divinity and humanity. He has humanity and
He also has divinity; He has divinity and He also has humanity. According to His divinity, He was born of the Holy Spirit;
according to His humanity, He was born of a human virgin.
Therefore, the Holy Spirit was not only in Him, but even
more, the Holy Spirit became the essence of His being.

Then we would ask: In Matthew 3, after the baptism of
the Lord Jesus while the Holy Spirit was outside of Him like
a dove in the air, did the Lord Jesus have the Holy Spirit
within Him? Without a doubt, the Lord Jesus had the
Holy Spirit within Him. Not only so, His very essence was

the Holy Spirit. Then are there two Holy Spirits, one being inside the Lord Jesus as His essence and another being outside, in the air, to descend upon Him? No, there is only one Holy Spirit. On the one hand, the Holy Spirit was in the Lord Jesus as His essence for His existence; this is the essential aspect. On the other hand, the Holy Spirit descended upon the Lord Jesus at the time of His baptism as the economical Spirit to be His power for His ministry; this is the economical aspect.

b. The Son Coming from and with the Father, and the Father Being Always with the Son

Among Christians there is also the concept that when the Lord Jesus came down from heaven because of His love for us, He left the Father on the throne in heaven, and He alone became flesh to be on the earth to suffer on our behalf; therefore, when He was suffering on the earth, the Father was far away in heaven. John 8:16, 29, and 16:32, however, strongly indicate that the Lord Jesus was never alone when He was on the earth; instead, the Father was always with Him. Furthermore, in 6:46; 7:29; 16:27; 17:8; and 15:26, five verses that refer to the Lord Jesus' coming from the Father, the Greek word for *from* is *para,* which means *from with.* This means that the Lord came not only from the Father but also with the Father. When He came from the Father, He brought the Father with Him.

Hence, when the Lord Jesus was on the earth, He came with the Father, and the Father was with Him. Thus, we would go on and ask: After His baptism, when He came out of the water and stood there, why did the Father speak from the heavens? Had the Father not already come with Him? Was not the Father always with Him? Then why is it that the Father was also in the heavens? Here we must see the two aspects concerning the Divine Trinity: the essential aspect and the economical aspect. According to the essential aspect, from the time the Lord Jesus entered Mary's womb, He came not only from the Father but also with the Father. According to the economical aspect, at His baptism the Father was still in the heavens.

c. The Father Being with the Son
in the Son's Crucifixion

While the Lord Jesus was being crucified, was the Father also there? Many fundamentalists do not dare to answer this question.

As early as the first century there rose up a heretical teacher, Cerinthus, who was a Syrian of Jewish descent. His heresy was a mixture of Judaism, Gnosticism, and Christianity. He separated the creator of the world from God and represented that creator as a subordinate power. He taught adoptionism, saying that Jesus was merely God's adopted Son and had become the Son of God by being exalted to a status that was not His by birth; thus, he denied that Jesus had been conceived by the Spirit. In his heresy he separated the earthly man Jesus, regarded as the son of Joseph and Mary, from the heavenly Christ and taught that after Jesus was baptized, Christ as a dove descended upon Him, and then He announced the unknown Father and did miracles. Furthermore, Cerinthus taught that at the end of His ministry Christ departed from Jesus, and Jesus suffered death on the cross and rose from the dead, while Christ remained separate as a spiritual being. Finally he also taught that Christ will rejoin the man Jesus at the coming of the Messianic kingdom of glory.

Cerinthus advocated that the One who was baptized and who died was Jesus, and the One who descended upon Him to be with Him was Christ. Christ was upon Jesus for only three and a half years to be His power and authority which enabled Him to perform miracles and wonders, to cast out demons and heal the sick, and to have spiritual wisdom. Then when Jesus went to the cross, Christ departed from Him. This is why Jesus prayed on the cross, "My God, My God, why have You forsaken Me?" (Matt. 27:46). This kind of teaching is a great heresy.

It is true that when the Lord Jesus was baptized, the Holy Spirit descended upon Him. And when He was crucified on the cross, at a certain time during those six hours the Holy Spirit did depart from Him; that is why He prayed, "My God,

My God, why have You forsaken Me?" (vv. 45-46). However, the descending and departing Spirit was not of the essential aspect but of the economical aspect. Economically, the Holy Spirit came and went, descended and departed; essentially, the Holy Spirit had never left the Lord Jesus from beginning to end but remained always as His essence.

Furthermore, it was not the Son alone who was born in the manger; rather, it was the Father accompanying the Son and being with the Son. In the same principle, the Son was not crucified alone on the cross, but the Father even accompanied the Son and was with the Son in the crucifixion. Therefore, the blood that was shed on the cross can be called "His [God's] own blood" through which the church was obtained (Acts 20:28). Furthermore, 1 John 1:7 says, "The blood of Jesus His [God's] Son cleanses us from every sin." This blood is not only the blood of Jesus but also the blood of God's Son. Therefore, Charles Wesley wrote in a hymn, saying, "Amazing love! how can it be / That Thou, my God, shouldst die for me?" (*Hymns,* #296). This means that not only did Jesus as a man die on the cross for us but that God also went through death in the man Jesus. Most fundamentalists dare not speak about this because they are afraid of being involved with heresy. However, the revelation of the Bible is clear: Essentially, the Father participated in the Lord's birth, sufferings, and death; economically, when the Lord was baptized, the Father was in the heavens, and when the Lord was crucified, the Father left Him. The Bible indeed reveals these two aspects.

4. The Economical Trinity

Concerning the Divine Trinity there are two aspects: the essential aspect and the economical aspect. The term economy means "arrangement," "plan," "administration," "management"; hence, it denotes moves, works, and doings. All of the Lord's moves, works, and doings belong to the economical aspect. Let us take incarnation as an example. The Bible does not say that the Lord Jesus became flesh or that the Son of God became flesh; it says that God became flesh. John 1 says that in the beginning was the Word, that the Word was God, and that the Word who was God became flesh (vv. 1, 14). First

Timothy 3:15 mentions God, and then verse 16 goes on to say, "And confessedly, great is the mystery of godliness: He who was manifested in the flesh." This shows us that the One who was manifested in the flesh is God. Hence, the Lord Jesus was God who became flesh; all the experiences of the Lord on the earth were God's experiences in Him. This is the essential aspect. However, in the economical aspect, when the Lord Jesus was baptized, the Father spoke to Him from the heavens; when He was crucified, the Father left Him. This is the economical aspect, the aspect of doings.

John 14 through 16 are the most mysterious as well as the most explicit chapters concerning the Divine Trinity. In these chapters the Lord spoke a clear message, saying, "He who has seen Me has seen the Father;...I am in the Father and the Father is in Me" (14:9-10). But in chapter seventeen He lifted up His eyes to heaven and prayed, "Father,..." (v. 1). Since he who has seen Him has seen the Father, and since He and the Father are one (10:30), He did not need to pray to the Father but could do whatever He wanted. Then why did He still pray to the Father? Furthermore, since the Father was in Him, why did He have to go such a long distance by lifting up His eyes to heaven instead of taking the shorter route by looking within Himself? Therefore, here we can see that there are two aspects concerning the Divine Trinity. The Son is in the Father, and the Father is in the Son; this is the essential aspect. The Son, who was on the earth, lifted up His eyes to heaven and prayed to the Father; this is the economical aspect. If you do not see these two aspects but instead hold on stubbornly to one aspect only, then you do not have a complete knowledge of the truth concerning the Divine Trinity.

Brothers and sisters, concerning the Divine Trinity, we should not debate blindly like the blind men feeling the elephant. Rather, we should have the knowledge of these two aspects, the essential aspect and the economical aspect. Thus, when we read the Bible, we will be able to see the complete revelation concerning the Divine Trinity, and we will also be able to see that the Bible is consistent, without any contradiction, in its revelation concerning the Divine Trinity.

CHAPTER THREE

CONCERNING THE DIVINE TRINITY

(3)

Scripture Reading: 1 Cor. 15:45b; 2 Cor. 3:17; Rev. 1:4; Isa. 9:6; Heb. 1:3; Col. 1:15; Rev. 5:6

OUTLINE

D. The creeds:
  1. The Apostles' Creed.
  2. The Nicene Creed.
  3. A Revision of the Nicene Creed.
  4. The Chalcedonian Confession of Faith.
  5. The Athanasian Creed.
  6. A heresy in the creeds—the Mother of God (*Theotokos*).
  7. The inadequacy of the creeds:
      a. The last Adam becoming the life-giving Spirit—1 Cor. 15:45b.
      b. The Lord being the Spirit—2 Cor. 3:17.
      c. The seven Spirits—Rev. 1:4; 3:1; 4:5; 5:6.
      d. The Son being called the Eternal Father—Isa. 9:6.
      e. The coinherence of the Father, the Son, and the Spirit—John 14:10, 20; 10:38; 17:21, 23.
      f. The Son being the effulgence of God's glory and the impress of God's substance—Heb. 1:3; Col. 1:15a; 2 Cor. 4:4.
      g. The Spirit being the eyes of the Son—Rev. 5:6; Zech. 3:9; 4:10.

    h. The Son as the Angel of Jehovah; as Jehovah, the self-existing and ever-existing One; and as Elohim, the Triune God—Exo. 3:2-15; 14:19; 23:20-21; Judg. 13:15-21; cf. Rev. 7:2; 8:3; 10:1; 18:1.

    i. The Son as the One sent by Jehovah and as Jehovah, the Sender—Zech. 2:8-11.

    j. When Christ, the Son, was baptized, the Spirit descending upon Him; when He died, God forsaking Him—Matt. 3:16; 27:46.

    k. The Son being the only begotten Son of the Father and the firstborn Son of God—John 1:18; 3:18; Rom. 8:29.

    l. The Son being the Firstborn of all creation—Col. 1:15b.

    m. The blood shed by the Son in His humanity being called the blood of God's Son and God's own blood—1 John 1:7; Acts 20:28.

    n. Christ being the mystery of God and in Him all the fullness of the entire Godhead—the Father, the Son, and the Spirit—dwelling bodily—Col. 2:2, 9.

    o. Christ, the Son, being the embodiment of the fullness of the divinity of the entire Triune God—Col. 2:9.

D. The Creeds

We have covered three crucial points concerning the Divine Trinity. Now we come to the fourth point—the creeds which have been highly regarded by the church through the ages for nearly two thousand years. A creed is a rule of faith. When the contents of man's belief are enumerated and set forth in writing, article by article, these articles of faith are called a creed. Due to man's inadequate knowledge, the creeds all have some deviations and defects. The outline above shows us one heresy found in the creeds and fifteen items lacking in the creeds.

Today's degraded and deformed Christianity puts the cart before the horse, so to speak, by taking the creeds instead of the entire body of biblical truths as the standard. This is a grave mistake. Although the creeds are good, they are incomplete and even considerably incomplete. In 1828 the Brethren were raised up by the Lord. After discovering the inadequacy of the creeds, they declared that they wanted no creed but the Bible. The incompleteness of the creeds is primarily due to the inadequate knowledge concerning the Divine Trinity. Following the Brethren, those in the Baptist denomination also declared, "No creed but the Bible." Then another group, the so-called Church of Christ, also made the same declaration. The fourth group of people to make such a declaration are those who are in the Lord's recovery. Sixty years ago when we were raised up in China, we also declared, "We do not care for the creeds; we care only for the Bible."

Concerning the doctrine of the Divine Trinity, there have been mainly three major schools through the centuries. The first school is the doctrine of the Trinity, which regards the Father, the Son, and the Spirit as the Triune God; this is based upon the pure revelation of the Scriptures. The second school is tritheism, which regards the Father, the Son, and the Spirit as three persons respectively with each One being a God; hence, the three are three Gods. The third school is modalism, the doctrine of God being one, which advocates that there is one God with three persons—the Father, the Son, and the Spirit—in three different stages. Both modalism and tritheism stress only one side of the truth; hence, both are heretical. The true balanced teaching is the doctrine of Trinity with the correct teaching concerning God's being uniquely one and yet distinctly three.

After I went to America, I began to release the truth concerning the Trinity according to the knowledge of the truth which we have obtained from the Bible. As a result, this has stirred up great oppositions. Over two hundred sixty publications, including periodicals and newspapers, were used by the opposing ones to attack me. We have been fighting for this truth since 1970. Eventually the opposing parties were subdued because the truth is the truth, and the more it is debated, the clearer it becomes. I have spent decades paying attention to this point. In reading every chapter and even every verse of the Bible, I would always pay attention to the matter of the Divine Trinity. Hence, I can say that we have studied every aspect of the Trinity revealed in the Bible. The most important study is in the Gospel of John and in Revelation. These two books reveal the mystery of the Divine Trinity in a very thorough manner.

Now we will briefly cover the five creeds.

1. The Apostles' Creed

According to church history, the earliest creed is the Apostles' Creed. This creed originated with a group of church fathers, who were all Bible scholars, in the beginning of the second century shortly after the passing away of the apostles. Based upon the apostles' teachings, they made a thorough study of the truth concerning the Triune God in the Bible in order to give a definition to the Divine Trinity. They were serious and accurate in their study, and the items they set forth may be considered quite deep, thorough, and detailed. The only shortcoming is the incompleteness of the contents. They should not be blamed for this because although the truth concerning the Divine Trinity has been revealed in the sixty-six books of the Bible in a way that is both mysterious and thorough, the items are scattered here and there; hence, it is not very easy to have an exhaustive study.

Next, in the age of the church fathers, seven books of the

New Testament had yet to be publicly recognized as authoritative. These books were Hebrews, James, 2 Peter, 2 John, 3 John, Jude, and Revelation. Although these seven books were widely read, there were still arguments concerning whether they could be counted as authoritative among the sacred writings and thus worthy of permanent recognition. It was not until A.D. 397 at the Council of Carthage in North Africa that these seven books were affirmed and recognized as a part of the New Testament.

Concerning the process of the formal recognition of the books of the Bible, the Old Testament canonization began at the time of Ezra and took more than four hundred years before it was finally completed at the beginning of the New Testament age. Then the New Testament canonization took another four hundred years for its completion. Therefore, it took almost eight hundred years for the canon of the entire Bible to be finalized. Today those who fear God, know God, and know the Bible all acknowledge that this recognition was undoubtedly of God's sovereignty. The apostles passed away before the completion of the New Testament canon. In the second century it was not easy for the first group of church fathers to give a complete definition of the Divine Trinity. Although they knew the Bible, they were still short of seven books in their hands. Nevertheless, they still produced the best piece of work. According to my study and research, all the items they set forth were accurate, penetrating, and thorough.

The main contents of the Apostles' Creed are as follows: "I believe in God the Father Almighty, Maker of heaven and earth. And in Jesus Christ His only Son our Lord....I believe in the Holy Ghost; the holy catholic Church; the communion of saints; the forgiveness of sins; the resurrection of the body; and the life everlasting. Amen." The Apostles' Creed declares that we believe "in Jesus Christ His only Son our Lord, who was conceived by the Holy Ghost, born of the virgin Mary, suffered under Pontius Pilate, was crucified, dead, and buried; He descended into Hades; the third day He rose again from the dead; He ascended into heaven, and sitteth on the right hand of God the Father Almighty; from thence He shall come to judge the quick and the dead."

2. The Nicene Creed

Although the Apostles' Creed was written in a simple way, it implies the considerable thoroughness of the research done by the church fathers and the great depth of their study of the Word. Following the Apostles' Creed is the Nicene Creed, which was instituted in the Council of Nicaea assembled by Constantine the Great in A.D. 325. In those days Christianity already had a great influence in the regions around the Mediterranean Sea which were under the control of the Roman Empire. However, the church leaders were in discord due to disputes concerning the truth; hence, there were divisions among them. At that time, although the Roman Empire ruled over the surrounding regions of the Mediterranean Sea, it was difficult to achieve unity due to the differences in nationalities, languages, and customs. During the reign of Constantine the Great, with his ambition and power he had the intention to rule over the Roman Empire to the extent of achieving unity not only politically but also religiously. He believed that the unity within territories of the Roman Empire hinged on the unity of the Christians because of their influential power within the empire. If the Christians could not be one, then there could not be oneness among the people of the Roman Empire. For this reason, he issued an edict to convene the Council of Nicaea. With himself acting as the moderator, he assembled all the bishops, the interpreters of the Bible, who were within the Roman Empire with the expectation of resolving the disputes regarding the truth.

In the assembly the bishops were urged by Constantine to present their opinions, and decisions were made based upon the Apostles' Creed. Eventually, the so-called Nicene Creed was instituted and its main contents are as follows: "I believe in one God the Father Almighty, Maker of all things, both visible and invisible. And in one Lord Jesus Christ....And in the Holy Ghost." The Nicene Creed asserts that we believe "in one Lord Jesus Christ, the Son of God, begotten of the Father, only begotten, that is of the substance of the Father,

God of God, Light of Light, very God of very God, begotten not made, of one substance with the Father, by whom all things were made, both those in heaven and those on earth; who for us men and for our salvation came down and was incarnate, was made Man, suffered, and rose the third day, ascended into heaven, is coming to judge the quick and dead."

We can see that the shortcoming of the Apostles' Creed was not corrected in the Nicene Creed. Furthermore, although the Nicene Creed contains no heresy and is actually not bad, it is still incomplete in its contents, since there were seven books that had not yet been authenticated as authoritative.

After the making of the Nicene Creed, it was recognized by the "catholic church," the predecessor of the Roman Catholic Church. Both the so-called catholic church and the Roman Catholic Church considered themselves as the unified and universal church; hence, it is called the "Catholic Church." To this day, the Roman Catholic Church still calls herself officially the "Catholic Church." Why is the Roman Catholic Church also called the "Church of the Lord of Heaven" among the Chinese? This is because when the Western missionaries came to China, they gave a great deal of consideration in the translation of the word *God*. They believed that the Chinese word *Shen* for *God* is ambiguous and thus cannot express the original meaning, so they decided to render *God* as *T'ien Chu,* the "Lord of heaven." Later, based upon this, people began to call the Roman Catholic Church *T'ien Chu Chiao,* the "Church of the Lord of Heaven." In my youth I saw *T'ien Chu T'ang,* the "hall of the Lord of Heaven," written on their place of worship; this proves that they also accepted this designation. However, they are not happy to be called the Romish Church.

After the Council of Nicaea, the Roman Empire was gradually divided politically into the Eastern Empire and the Western Empire. The capital of the Western Empire was the city of Rome; the capital of the Eastern Empire was Constantinople, situated at the border of Europe and Asia, and is called Istanbul today. It was built up by Constantine as the eastern capital of the Roman Empire. After the division of the Roman Empire, the Catholic Church was also divided into the Eastern Orthodox Church and the western Roman Catholic Church. Besides the political factor, the division was also caused by a strong controversy involving the Divine Trinity. Apparently, the reason for division was that the Eastern Orthodox Church would not recognize the authority of the Pope of the Roman Catholic Church; actually, the intrinsic reason was the theological dispute. The Eastern Orthodox Church would not admit that they teach tritheism, yet according to the grounds of their arguments, they were actually teaching tritheism. The Roman Catholic Church is superior, in a sense, in that they believe in the Triune God.

3. A Revision of the Nicene Creed

In A.D. 381, fifty-six years after the Nicene Council, those who used the Nicene Creed felt that its statements were oversimplified, not being detailed enough. Therefore, they revised its contents, added some new items to it, and called it "A Revision of the Nicene Creed." The main contents of this creed are as follows: "I believe in one God the Father Almighty, Maker of heaven and earth, and of all things visible and invisible. And in one Lord Jesus Christ....And I believe in the Holy Ghost, the Lord, and Giver of life; who proceedeth from the Father; who with the Father and the Son together is worshipped and glorified; who spake by the Prophets. And I believe in the one holy catholic and apostolic Church; I acknowledge one baptism for the remission of sins; and I look for the resurrection of the dead, and the life of the world to come."

The revised Nicene Creed declared that we believe "in one Lord Jesus Christ, the only-begotten Son of God, begotten of the Father before all worlds; God of God, Light of Light, very God of very God, begotten, not made, being of one substance with the Father; by whom all things were made; who, for us men, and for our salvation, came down from heaven, and was incarnate by the Holy Ghost of the Virgin Mary, and was made man; and was crucified also for us under Pontius Pilate; he suffered and was buried; and the third day He rose again, according to the Scriptures; and ascended into heaven, and sitteth on the right hand of the Father; and He shall come again, with glory, to judge both the quick and the dead; whose kingdom shall have no end."

However, even though this revised creed is richer than the earlier Nicene Creed in contents and likewise contains no error or heresy, it is still incomplete in that seven books of the New Testament had yet to be recognized.

4. The Chalcedonian Confession of Faith

In A.D. 397, in the third general Council, held at Carthage in North Africa, the final seven books of the New Testament were officially recognized. In A.D. 451, the emperor of Rome convoked the fourth general Council of Chalcedonia. Chalcedonia and Constantinople were sister cities separated only by a strait. In this Council, the contents of the Nicene Creed were greatly increased to make the original Creed more exhaustive. The result was a new creed called "The Chalcedonian Confession of Faith"; its contents are as follows: "Following the holy fathers, we unanimously teach one and the same Son, our Lord Jesus Christ, complete as to his Godhead, and complete as to his manhood; truly God, and truly man, of a reasonable [rational] soul and human flesh subsisting; consubstantial with the Father as to his Godhead, and consubstantial also with us as to his manhood; like unto us in all things, yet without sin; as to his Godhead begotten of the Father before all worlds, but as to his manhood, in these last days born, for us men and for our salvation, of the Virgin Mary, the Mother of God; one and the same Christ, Son, Lord, Only-begotten, known in (of) two natures, without confusion, without conversion, without severance, and without division; the distinction of the natures being in no wise abolished by their union, but the peculiarity of each nature being maintained, and both concurring in one person and hypostasis. We confess not a Son divided and sundered into two persons, but one and the same Son, and Only-begotten, and God-Logos, our Lord Jesus Christ, even as the prophets had before proclaimed concerning him, and he himself hath taught us, and the symbol of the fathers hath handed down to us."

However, the expansion of the contents brought in a great heresy. Concerning the origin of the Lord Jesus Christ, the adopters of this creed stated that "as to his manhood, in these last days born, for us men and for our salvation, of the Virgin Mary, the Mother of God." This means that they consider-ed Mary "the Mother of God"; this is truly a great heresy.

5. The Athanasian Creed

Now we come to the fifth creed, the Athanasian Creed. This creed was attributed to Athanasius, though it was not written by him. Athanasius was an attendant of the Nicene Council who served as an assistant (comparable to today's secretary) to one of the bishops who participated in the Coun-cil. He became famous, however, for speaking out against the teachings of the great heretic Arius. Arius erroneously taught that Christ was not the eternal God but an extraordinary, noble man who was later deified by God. Furthermore, Arius also had a wrong understanding of Colossians 1:15 and main-tained that Christ is not the Creator since He is the Firstborn of all creation. This is a great heresy. Hence, in that council Arius encountered severe oppositions and thenceforth was condemned and exiled abroad. Because Athanasius was the most powerful antagonist of the Arians, some considered the creed adopted by the Nicene Council as his writing.

From then on the creed had been revised and expanded again and again until A.D. 553, when a creed that was richer and more exhaustive than the previous ones was produced. This creed was called "The Athanasian Creed," and its con-tents are as follows:

1. Whosoever will be saved, before all things it is necessary that he hold the catholic faith.
2. Which faith except every one do keep whole and undefiled, without doubt he shall perish everlast-ingly.
3. But this is the catholic faith: That we worship one God in trinity, and trinity in unity;
4. Neither confounding the persons: nor dividing the substance.
5. For there is one person of the Father: another of the Son: and another of the Holy Ghost.
6. But the Godhead of the Father, and of the Son, and

of the Holy Ghost is all one: the glory equal, the majesty co-eternal.

7. Such as the Father is, such is the Son, and such is the Holy Ghost.

8. The Father is uncreated: the Son is uncreated: and the Holy Ghost is uncreated.

9. The Father is immeasurable: the Son is immeasurable: the Holy Ghost is immeasurable.

10. The Father eternal: the Son eternal: and the Holy Ghost eternal.

11. And yet there are not three eternals; but one eternal.

12. As also there are not three uncreated: nor three immeasurable, but one uncreated: and one immeasurable.

13. So likewise the Father is almighty: the Son almighty: and the Holy Ghost almighty.

14. And yet there are not three Almighties: but one Almighty.

15. So the Father is God: the Son is God: and the Holy Ghost is God.

16. And yet there are not three Gods; but one God.

17. So the Father is Lord: the Son Lord: and the Holy Ghost Lord.

18. And yet not three Lords; but one Lord.

19. For like as we are compelled by the Christian verity to acknowledge every Person by himself to be God and Lord:

20. So are we forbidden by the catholic religion to say, there are three Gods, or three Lords.

21. The Father is made of none; neither created; nor begotten.

22. The Son is of the Father alone: not made; nor created; but begotten.

23. The Holy Ghost is of the Father and the Son: neither made; neither created; nor begotten; but proceeding.

24. Thus there is one Father, not three Fathers: one Son, not three Sons: one Holy Ghost, not three Holy Ghosts.

25. And in this Trinity none is before or after another: none is greater or less than another.
26. But the whole three Persons are co-eternal, and co-equal.
27. So that in all things, as aforesaid, the Unity in Trinity, and the Trinity in Unity, is to be worshipped.
28. He therefore that will be saved, must thus think of the Trinity.
29. Furthermore it is necessary to everlasting salvation, that we believe also rightly in the Incarnation of our Lord Jesus Christ.
30. Now the right faith is, that we believe and confess, that our Lord Jesus Christ, the Son of God, is God and Man.
31. God, of the substance of the Father, begotten before the worlds: and Man, of the substance of his mother, born in the world.
32. Perfect God: and perfect Man, of a reasonable soul and human flesh subsisting.
33. Equal to the Father as touching His Godhead: inferior to the Father as touching his Manhood.
34. Who although He be God and Man; yet He is not two, but one Christ.
35. One; not by conversion of the Godhead into flesh; but by assumption of the Manhood into God.
36. One altogether, not by confusion of substance; but by unity of person.
37. For as the reasonable soul and flesh is one man; so God and Man is one Christ.
38. Who suffered for our salvation: descended into hades: rose again the third day from the dead.
39. He ascended into heaven: He sitteth on the right hand of the Father God, the Father almighty:
40. From whence He shall come to judge the quick and the dead.
41. At whose coming all men must rise again with their bodies;
42. And shall give account for their own works.
43. And they that have done good shall go into life

everlasting; but they that have done evil, into everlasting fire.

44. This is the catholic faith; which except a man believe
truly and firmly, he cannot be saved.

Glory to the Father, the Son, and the Holy Ghost. So
it was, and is, and ever shall be, without end forever.
Amen.

6. A Heresy in the Creeds—the Mother of God

Now we come to the heresy in the creeds—the Mother of
God (*Theotokos*). Earlier we said that this heresy was
recorded in the Chalcedonian Confession of Faith adopted
in A.D. 451. In Greek, *Theo* means "God," and *tokos* means
"bearer"; hence, *Theotokos* is rendered "the Mother of God."
This is a great heresy, for how can the eternal God have a
finite human being of flesh as His "Mother"? Perhaps some
may argue that the mention of "the Mother of God" is related
to Christ's humanity. Yes, according to His humanity, He had
a mother, but we cannot say that this mother is "the Mother
of God."

Theological studies throughout the ages concluded, based
upon the Bible, that our Lord Jesus is indeed the complete
God who came in the flesh to become a perfect man. His
divinity is complete and His humanity is perfect. As God, He
possesses divinity; as a man, He possesses humanity. According to His humanity, Mary is His mother; but we cannot
say that Mary is His mother in His divinity. We can only say
that Mary is the mother of the man Jesus; we cannot say that
Mary is the Mother of God.

The Lord Jesus is God, not a partial God, but the complete
God. He is neither just one part of the Triune God nor just
one-third of God. He is God (Rom. 9:5), not only God the Son
but the complete God—the Father, the Son, and the Spirit
(cf. Isa. 9:6; John 14:9; 1 Cor. 15:45b; 2 Cor. 3:17). Furthermore, the Lord Jesus is also a perfect man. Just as man has a
spirit, He also has a spirit (John 11:33); just as man has
a soul, He also has a soul (Matt. 26:38); just as man has a
body, He also has a body (John 2:21). Since He has humanity,
it was necessary that He have a mother for the human birth.

Hence, Mary is His mother in His humanity but not His mother in His divinity. Therefore, we cannot call Mary "the Mother of God."

This heresy led to a great dispute in the Roman Catholic Church concerning the matter of whether Mary had "original sin." This dispute lasted over fourteen hundred years. Then in the 1850s it was officially determined by the Pope that Mary did not have original sin. This is a great heresy. This point has become a strong factor of our refusal to accept the creeds. We admit that the major part of the creeds is right, yet they contain such a great heresy in the statement, recorded in plain words, concerning "the Mother of God."

7. The Inadequacy of the Creeds

Besides the heresy about "the Mother of God," there are no other gross errors in the creeds; in fact, many of the items in the creeds are quite accurate. Nevertheless, all the creeds, besides containing some errors, are incomplete. Hence, they cannot be our rules of faith but can serve only as references. For over fifty to sixty years I myself have directly received a great deal from the Bible by finding out the truths, item by item, contained in it. By the spring of 1983, what I found was nearly complete. Then when I spent time to refer to the creeds, I discovered that many items in the creeds are similar to what we have seen, yet I also found out that the creeds are short of many items. In the following paragraphs I will enumerate and briefly discuss fifteen items that are missing in the creeds. I hope that you will be able to understand and enter into them and even apply and speak them.

a. The Last Adam
Becoming the Life-giving Spirit

First Corinthians 15:45b says that "the last Adam became a life-giving Spirit." The omission of this point is the greatest defect of the creeds. The Bible tells us that the Lord Jesus is the Word who was in the beginning and that the Word became flesh; in the flesh He is the last Adam. In God's eyes the Lord Jesus is the last man and, as such, He concludes the adamic race. Through His death and resurrection He became the life-giving Spirit. This is a very great matter. Today after having read through the Bible and having some amount of experience, we have this conclusion: this life-giving Spirit is the ultimate consummation of the Triune God.

b. The Lord Being the Spirit

Second Corinthians 3:17 says that "the Lord is the Spirit." The creeds have neglected this point. The proponents of tritheism say that "the Lord" here is actually "God," who is generally referred to as "the Lord." However, if we read 2 Corinthians chapters one through four, we must admit that "the Lord" mentioned in 3:17 is the Lord who died and resurrected and who has been made both Lord and Christ. The sentence "the Lord is the Spirit" was written as a continuation of "the last Adam became a life-giving Spirit." Now the Lord, who died, resurrected, and ascended to heaven, is the Spirit. This point has not been mentioned in any of the creeds. Yet in the New Testament, in particular in the Epistles written by Paul, it has been thoroughly disclosed (Rom. 8:16, 23, 26-27; Gal. 3:2, 5, 14; 6:8).

c. The Seven Spirits

The third shortcoming of the creeds is that they do not mention the seven Spirits. Revelation 1:4; 3:1; 4:5; and 5:6 all mention the seven Spirits. We cannot blame the Nicene Creed for not referring to the seven Spirits, since the book of Revelation had yet to be recognized at that time. However, after the recognition of Revelation in A.D. 397, the point concerning the seven Spirits was not added to either the Chalcedonian Confession of Faith or the Athanasian Creed. This indicates either that the people at that time did not see it or that they did not value or understand it and therefore did not dare to touch it or speak about it. However, this is a matter of great significance because it is mentioned in the last book of the Bible as a conclusion. In this conclusion, the Spirit of God has become the seven Spirits.

d. The Son Being Called the Eternal Father

Isaiah 9:6 says, "For a child is born to us, / A son is given to us;... / And His name will be called... / Mighty God, / Eternal Father." The orthodox Bible expositors all acknowledge that the "child" here refers to the Lord Jesus, whose name would be called the Mighty God, and that the "son," of course, refers to the second of the Divine Trinity, yet His name would be called the Eternal Father. This item is of great importance in settling the truth concerning the Divine Trinity, yet it is also omitted from the creeds.

e. The Coinherence of the Father, the Son, and the Spirit

In the text of five verses in John, the Lord Jesus repeatedly said, "I am in the Father and the Father is in Me" (14:10, 20; 10:38; 17:21, 23). This shows that the Son coinheres with the Father. In John 8:29 the Lord said, "He who sent Me is with Me." Also, Luke 4:1 says that "Jesus, full of the Holy Spirit." These verses prove that when the Son was living on the earth, the Father and the Spirit were with Him; the three were coinherent and not separated. This item, which is crucial to the truth concerning the Divine Trinity, is only implied but not clearly mentioned in the creeds.

f. The Son Being the Effulgence of God's Glory and the Impress of God's Substance

Hebrews 1:3 says that the Lord Jesus is "the effulgence of His [God's] glory and the impress of His substance." Colossians 1:15a and 2 Corinthians 4:4 both mention that Christ, the Son of God's love, is the image of God. Since the Son is the image of God, how can we say that the image of God is one person and the Father is another person? Are your image and you one or two? Can you say that a certain brother's face and the brother himself are two? That the Lord is the Spirit, that the Son is called the Eternal Father, and that the Son is the image of the Father—all these truths are extremely important yet they are lacking in the creeds.

g. The Spirit Being the Eyes of the Son

In Zechariah 3:9 and 4:10 and in Revelation 5:6 we can see

that the "stone" and the "Lamb" both refer to the Lord Jesus and that the "seven eyes" upon the stone and of the Lamb refer to the seven Spirits of God; hence, the Spirit is the eyes of the Son.

The proponents of tritheism assert that the Father, the Son, and the Spirit are three persons, each One standing alone. The Bible, however, says that the Son is the image of the Father and the Spirit is the eyes of the Son. This is too marvelous. It is true that the image and the person are distinct, but they cannot be separated; likewise, the eyes and the person are distinct but inseparable. The image is for expression, and the eyes are for transmission. The Son as the image of the Father expresses the Father; whereas the Spirit as the eyes of this "image" transmits the Son. Hence, the three—the Father, the Son, and the Spirit—are distinct, just as a person himself, his image, and his eyes are distinctly three. Yet the three are one and cannot be divided. This is where the mystery of the Triune God lies.

h. The Son as the Angel of Jehovah; as Jehovah, the Self-existing and Ever-existing One; and as Elohim, the Triune God

The Angel of Jehovah mentioned in Exodus and Judges is the Son (Exo. 3:2-15; 14:19; 23:20-21; Judg. 13:15-21). We say this because in Revelation the Lord Jesus is referred to as "another Angel" (7:2; 8:3; 10:1; 18:1). If we carefully study Exodus 3, we will discover that the Angel of Jehovah who appeared to Moses in a flame of fire out of the thornbush is Jehovah, the self-existing and ever-existing One (v. 14). Self-existing and ever-existing means "I AM WHO I AM." As such, He is the One "who is and who was and who is coming" (Rev. 1:4), the One who is self-existing, ever-existing, immeasurable, and without beginning or ending. In Matthew 1, this Jehovah became Jesus. *Jesus* means "Jehovah the Savior," or "the salvation of Jehovah." This is why we say that the Son is Jehovah, the self-existing and ever-existing One. Exodus 3:6 goes on to say that Jehovah God is "the God of Abraham, the God of Isaac, and the God of Jacob." The Hebrew word for *God* here is *Elohim,* the Triune God. Therefore, this proves that the Son is also Elohim, the Triune God. This matter is not mentioned in the creeds.

i. The Son as the One Sent by Jehovah and as Jehovah, the Sender

In Zechariah 2:8-11 we see that the Lord Jesus is the One who was sent by Jehovah, and He is also Jehovah who sent Him. This portion of the Word was spoken by "Jehovah of hosts" (v. 8). Yet in this portion Jehovah of hosts said, "Jehovah of hosts has sent Me" (vv. 9, 11). This is to say that it is Jehovah of hosts who sent Jehovah of hosts. Furthermore, according to the original text, the pronoun *My* in verse 11 may also be rendered *His,* and the pronoun *I* may also be rendered *He.* This means that I am He and He is I. He is the sent One and the Sender. Hence, the sent One and the Sender are one. The tritheists believe that there are three Gods because they have not seen this point.

j. When Christ, the Son, Was Baptized, the Spirit Descending upon Him; When He Died, God Forsaking Him

It is recorded in Matthew 3:16 that when the Lord Jesus came out of the water after His baptism, the Spirit of God descended like a dove and came upon Him. Essentially, the Lord Jesus was born of the Holy Spirit and therefore already had the Spirit within Him. Yet it says here that the Spirit of God descended upon Him; this refers to the economical aspect. Furthermore, it is recorded in Matthew 27:46 that when the Lord Jesus was being crucified, He cried out with a loud voice, saying, "My God, My God, why have You forsaken Me?" Essentially, the Father was always with the Lord, not only while He was moving on the earth but even while He was being crucified. Therefore, the Bible says that the blood shed by the Lord Jesus on the cross is the blood of God's Son (1 John 1:7), and it is also God's own blood (Acts 20:28). As to the record in Matthew 27 concerning God's forsaking the Lord Jesus, it refers to the economical aspect. The creeds are also short in this matter.

k. The Son Being
the Only Begotten Son of the Father
and the Firstborn Son of God

The Son is the only begotten Son of the Father and the firstborn Son of God. Since the Son is the only begotten Son, He should not have any brothers; how then can He be also the firstborn Son? The Lord Jesus was the only begotten Son of God (John 1:18; 3:18; 1 John 4:9), but in His incarnation He partook of man's blood and flesh. The human nature and human flesh which He put on to become the Son of Man did not have divinity. Hence, in His incarnation, according to His divinity He was the only begotten Son of God, but according to His humanity He was the Son of Man and not the Son of God. Then He passed through death. When He died on the cross, His flesh died, but His Spirit as His divinity was made alive, enlivened, with new power of life (1 Pet. 3:18), and even His flesh which had been put to death was also made alive and resurrected, thereby bringing His humanity into divinity. Hence, His resurrection was a birth to Him in His humanity. On the day of resurrection, God said to Him, "This day have I begotten You" (Acts 13:33).

His incarnation was a birth; that was divinity putting on humanity. His resurrection was another birth; that was humanity putting on divinity. When He was crucified, not only He died, but all those who were chosen by God and who believe in Him died with Him in His death. Likewise, when He was resurrected, not only He was resurrected, but all those who have been chosen by God and who believe in Him were resurrected with Him in His resurrection, that is, were begotten with Him as sons of God (cf. 1 Pet. 1:3). In this way He obtained many brothers and became the firstborn Son.

Therefore, on the morning of His resurrection the Lord Jesus could say to Mary, "Go to My brothers and say to them, I ascend to My Father and your Father, and My God and your God" (John 20:17). Previously, as the only begotten Son He did not have brothers; in the morning of His resurrection, He had brothers because He had become the firstborn Son. One of the results of His resurrection is that His Father became the

Father of the believers. Thus, the Son became the Firstborn among many brothers (Rom. 8:29).

We must see clearly that as the only begotten Son the Son has divinity but does not have humanity, and that as the firstborn Son of God the Son has not only divinity but also humanity. The creeds are also short of this item.

l. The Son Being the Firstborn of All Creation

According to the humanity of the Son, the Bible says that He is a creature. Colossians 1:15b says the Son of God's love is "the Firstborn of all creation." Our critics have made a big mistake because they think that we speak about this matter according to the teaching of the Arians. In the book entitled *Concerning the Person of Christ* we have clearly said, "According to the complete revelation of the Bible, Christ is both the Creator and the creature, because He is God and He is man—He is God who creates, He is also man who is created....When Christ became a creature He did not lose His eternal, uncreated nature—He remains the Creator. In like manner, when He became man He did not lose His divine nature—He is still God" (pp. 45, 47).

Moreover, if we do not confess that Christ is a creature, this is equivalent to not confessing that Christ is God who "became flesh" (John 1:14) and "partook" of "blood and flesh" (Heb. 2:14) to become a "man" (1 Tim. 2:5). Then we would become Docetists (cf. 1 John 4:3, note 1, in *The New Testament, Recovery Version*). The Docetists believed that Christ only has divinity and does not have humanity, that His human body was not a real body but was merely a phantom. As referred to in 1 John 4:2-3, they did not confess that Christ came in the flesh.

Over thirty years ago, a so-called co-worker told me that Christ in heaven today is not a man. What he meant is that the Lord lost His human nature immediately after His resurrection and is therefore no longer a man. But Acts 7 says that Stephen, before he was stoned to death, saw the Lord Jesus still standing as the Son of Man at the right hand of God (v. 56). In Revelation 1, the apostle John saw that the Lord Jesus, who is walking in the midst of the golden lampstands, is like the Son of Man (v. 13). In Matthew 26, when the high priest interrogated the Lord Jesus, saying, "Tell us if You are the Christ, the Son of God" (v. 63), the Lord replied, "You will see the Son of Man sitting at the right hand of Power and coming on the clouds of heaven" (v. 64). This indicates that the Lord will still be the Son of Man at His coming back. Furthermore, John 1:51 proves that, in eternity, this Jesus will still be the Son of Man, on whom the angels of God will be ascending and descending. Hence, the Lord Jesus not only put on human nature when He became flesh, but He also died, resurrected, and ascended with His humanity, and He will have His humanity even in His coming back and unto eternity.

Some may ask, "Was it not only two thousand years ago that Christ became flesh? Why then does the Bible say that He is the Firstborn of all creation?" We need to consider this question not according to man's calculation but according to God's calculation. For example, according to man's calculation, the first man is Adam and the second man is Cain. However, the Bible says that the first man is Adam and the second man is Christ (1 Cor. 15:45-47); this is God's calculation.

Furthermore, Genesis 18:1 says that Jehovah appeared to Abraham, and then it says that Abraham saw three men coming. Among the three men, one was Jehovah. At Abraham's time Jehovah had not yet become flesh, yet He appeared to Abraham in the form of man. Abraham not only fetched water for Him to wash His feet (v. 4) but also served Him a meal (v. 8). That One was Christ with a human body, not a phantom. Therefore, in John 8 the Lord Jesus said, "Abraham exulted that he would see My day, and he saw it and rejoiced....Before Abraham came into being, I am" (vv. 56, 58). The creeds are also short of this point.

m. The Blood Shed by the Son in His Humanity
Being Called the Blood of God's Son
and God's Own Blood

First John 1:7 says, "The blood of Jesus His Son cleanses us from every sin." The name *Jesus* denotes the Lord's humanity, which is needed for the shedding of the redeeming blood. The title *His Son* denotes the Lord's divinity, which is needed for the eternal efficacy of the redeeming blood. Hence, Acts 20:28 says that the church was obtained by God "through His own blood."

n. Christ Being the Mystery of God and in Him All the Fullness of the Entire Godhead— the Father, the Son, and the Spirit—Dwelling Bodily

Colossians 2:2 says that Christ is the mystery of God. Then verse 9 says, "For in Him dwells all the fullness of the Godhead bodily." This means that the fullness of the entire Godhead—the Father, the Son, and the Spirit—dwells in Christ as one who has a human body. Before Christ's incarnation, the fullness of the Godhead dwelt in Him as the eternal Word (John 1:1), but not bodily. From the time that Christ became incarnate, clothed with a human body, the fullness of the Godhead began to dwell in Him in a bodily way; and in His glorified body (Phil. 3:21) now and forever it dwells.

o. Christ, the Son, Being the Embodiment of the Fullness of the Divinity of the Entire Triune God

The last item which the creeds are short of is the matter of Christ, the Son, being the embodiment of the fullness of the divinity of the entire Triune God. Hence, it is neither secure nor accurate enough to take only the creeds as the standard.

A CONCLUDING WORD

When we put together all these items that are omitted in the creeds, we can see that the Divine Trinity is indeed a mystery. The more we study the matter of the Trinity, the more we have to admit that the Trinity is truly mysterious and incomprehensible. This is why Martin Luther said that if you try to understand the matter concerning the Triune God, you will be the teacher of God. In this matter we all must say, "I have not yet come to know as I ought to know" (cf. 1 Cor. 8:2). If you say you know, then you are the teacher of God. Because the items concerning the Triune God are too mysterious, after we have thoroughly studied them, we have to humbly bow our heads in worship, saying, "Lord, how we thank You that in all these years You have released all these mysteries concerning the Divine Trinity in order that we may know how to enjoy You." If we are only for doctrinal study, we cannot adequately explain even an ordinary fish, let alone the Triune God. The Triune God is too mysterious. In conclusion, He is the Triune God; He has the aspect of being three, yet He is still one.

Recently, a group of people in America declared that they will go back to the Councils. This means that they believe that all issues must be decided according to the resolutions of the Councils and not according to the Bible. However, the resolutions of the Councils are simply the creeds; therefore, their intention is to go back to the creeds that are seriously short. For this reason, there is an undercurrent hidden here today and there is also a warfare. If you desire to serve the Lord full time for a long time, you must have the fundamental knowledge concerning this matter. What I have given you is just a sketch to show you that our knowledge of God is altogether scriptural and that most Christians' knowledge of God is mostly according to the creeds and is therefore inadequate. Even to this day they still recite the creeds during their worship in their worshipping places. The basis of their belief is the creeds instead of the Bible. However, the foundation of our faith is not the creeds. Rather, we study the Bible daily. This is our faith and our practice.

CONCERNING THE DIVINE TRINITY

(4)

Scripture Reading: Col. 2:2, 9; Isa. 9:6; 2 Cor. 3:17; John 1:14; Heb. 2:14; Col. 1:15, 18; Acts 2:36

OUTLINE

E. The all-inclusiveness of Christ:
  1. In His divinity:
     a. He is the mystery of God, and in Him all the fullness of the entire Godhead—the Father, the Son, and the Spirit—dwells bodily.
     b. He comes in the name of the Father and works also in the name of the Father.
     c. His name is called the Eternal Father.
     d. He is the image of God to declare God.
     e. In His name the Father sends the Holy Spirit, and in His name also the Holy Spirit comes.
     f. He sends the Holy Spirit from and with the Father, and the Holy Spirit also comes from and with the Father.
     g. He is the Spirit.
     h. He is the One who fills all in all.
  2. In His humanity:
     a. He became flesh, partaking of blood and flesh and taking the likeness of the flesh of sin.
     b. He became a man.
     c. He is the Firstborn of all creation.

  d. He is the Firstborn from the dead.

  e. He became the life-giving Spirit in resurrection.

  f. The Spirit of God became His Spirit, the Spirit of Jesus Christ.

  g. He poured out the Holy Spirit whom He had received from the Father, and He gives the Spirit not by measure.

  h. He was begotten with His humanity in resurrection to be the firstborn Son of God with many brothers.

  i. He was made both Lord and Christ in ascension.

  j. He is the Heir of all things.

E. The All-inclusiveness of Christ

In the preceding chapters we have already covered four points concerning the Divine Trinity: the revelation in the Bible—the Father, the Son, and the Spirit; theological expressions used through the centuries with regard to the Divine Trinity; four crucial points concerning the Divine Trinity; and the creeds. In this chapter we will see the fifth point concerning the Divine Trinity, that is, the all-inclusiveness of Christ, including eight items in His divinity and ten items in His humanity. I hope that you can spend more time to get into these eighteen points.

Beginning with the second century, there were many disputes among Christians concerning the Divine Trinity and the Person of Christ. For this reason, a number of councils were convened to settle the controversies, and as a result, the so-called creeds were brought forth. In the previous chapter we covered several of the creeds which were translated into Chinese through the joint efforts of some Western missionaries and Chinese Christians over fifty years ago. As a whole, the concepts incorporated in most of the creeds, whether in their original texts or in their translations into various languages, may be considered accurate. However, a great heresy concerning Mary being "the Mother of God" was added to the Chalcedonian Confession of Faith.

The Chalcedonian Confession of Faith also says that the Son is "consubstantial" with the Father. The Greek word for *consubstantial* is *homoousios: homo* means "same," "identical," and *ousios* means "essence of the substance" or "element." This means that the Father, the Son, and the Spirit are three persons, but instead of having three similar essences, They have the same one essence. This was a great point of dispute, because at that time there was another group of teachers who believed that the Father, the Son, and the Spirit have three *similar* elements; this means that although Their elements are similar, the three are three different persons. These teachers inserted the letter *i* in the middle of the Greek word for *consubstantial* to make it *homoiousios,* meaning "similar essences." Since the three of the Godhead have three similar essences, They are three separate existences. This developed into tritheism. Concerning this matter, what is advocated in the Chalcedonian Confession of Faith is in agreement with the Bible, and it is also what we have acknowledged; that is, the Divine Trinity has not merely similar essences but the same one essence. In other words, the essence that is in the first is also in the second and in the third; the three do not just have similar elements; They share the same element.

Therefore, as a whole the creeds are correct, but the heresy concerning "the Mother of God" is a great deviation. The practice of the Roman Catholic Church is to add a little leaven to the truth so that eventually the whole lump is leavened (cf. Matt. 13:33). If you read their teachings, in the end you will be poisoned.

We have spent much time commenting about these matters to show you that in the entire Christianity today, including both the Catholic Church and the Protestant churches, people trust in the creeds more than the Bible. A brother said that when he was studying in an elementary school founded by the Episcopalian Church in Hong Kong, all the students were required to recite the Apostles' Creed and the Nicene Creed during the weekly assemblies. He did not understand what was meant by "God of God, Light of Light, very God of very God." The Chinese translation then was not accurate, but even if it were properly translated, it is still hard to understand what this sentence means. Christianity honors the creeds to such an extent that concerning the persons of the Divine Trinity, instead of saying that this is what the Bible says, they would say that this is what the creeds say. The Catholics even would say that this is what the Catholic Church says. Their so-called church is their Pope. The Catholics in the whole world have to speak according to every decree or regulation given by the Pope. Thus, although they have the Bible, they put it aside. Hence, they not only have heresies but also have many defects.

The Subjective Knowledge of the Divine Trinity

I hope that you will earnestly make an effort in the training to learn all these matters. However, we are not ascetics in the Catholic Church. Many monasteries were established after the formation of the Catholic Church to teach people how to learn the truth by self-mortification. I do not want this training to be like a monastery, just teaching you how to suffer and to meditate. Otherwise, without the Triune God wrought into you, even if you have learned all the tasks and can do them well, you will still gain nothing. You must learn to put yourself aside that you may be filled with the Triune God.

I hope that all of you will know the Triune God and be constituted with and saturated by Him. Thus, when you go to visit people by door-knocking, it is the Triune God who goes with love, light, life, the Spirit, power, holiness, and righteousness, as well as with the gospel of grace, the gospel of the forgiveness of sins, the gospel of the kingdom, and the all-inclusive gospel. The gospel in the Bible is the processed Triune God. Today when we go forth to preach the gospel and to feed people, we are just like mothers nursing their children, but instead of carrying bottles of milk powder that are not part of us, we bring the milk that is in our intrinsic being. This is my burden. I hope you are clear that I have no intention or interest for you to go and debate with people. Rather, what I am doing here is to give you a disinfecting injection and an inoculation.

Today, you young brothers and sisters have risen up to love the Lord, and you have a desire to forsake all things for the Lord's recovery in the last days and to offer up everything you have. This is why I have to make this matter clear to you. This is the basic problem of Christianity. They are short of a total of eighteen items concerning the divinity and humanity of Christ; these items are not mentioned in their creeds. How can the Triune God be explained clearly by just a few, simple words of the creeds? We have published in books the results of our sixty years of studying the Bible and respectfully present them before you. I hope that the believers who have a seeking heart will give an objective and fair judgment by putting aside their past concepts and prejudices; then they will know that we are speaking biblical truths.

1. In His Divinity

a. He Is the Mystery of God, and in Him
All the Fullness of the Entire Godhead—
the Father, the Son, and the Spirit—Dwells Bodily

Colossians 2:2 says that Christ is the mystery of God. What is a mystery? A mystery is a story that is beyond human comprehension. That Christ is the mystery of God means that Christ is the story, the history, of God. Therefore, Colossians 2:9 says, "For in Him [Christ] dwells all the fullness of the Godhead bodily." Furthermore, 1:19 says, "For in Him all the fullness was pleased to dwell." *All the fullness of the Godhead* refers to all that the entire Triune God—the Father, the Son, and the Spirit—is, has, can do, has done, has obtained, has accomplished, and has attained; all of this fullness dwells in Christ bodily. Hence, Christ is the embodiment of the Triune God.

Today under the influence of the creeds, the speaking in Christianity concerning the Divine Trinity either leans toward tritheism or is very close to tritheism. There is a brother who worked with Brother Nee and me for over twenty years when we were in mainland China. In 1934 when the publication of *The Christian* was resumed and I was charged by Brother Nee to bear the editing responsibility, this co-worker also contributed articles to the magazine. However, in 1958 he condemned me, saying that I teach heresy when I say that "the Son is called the Father and that the Son is the Spirit." One of our senior co-workers went to have a talk with him, telling him that if this were a heresy, then it did not start with me but with Brother Nee, who had written a hymn with these lines: "Thou, Lord, the Father once wast called, / But now the Holy Spirit art" (*Hymns,* #490, stanza 5). That brother's reply was that Brother Nee could also be wrong. I felt then that that brother was not only short in his knowledge of the Bible but also inconsistent in his words and actions.

Then in 1965 while I was living in Los Angeles, this brother arrived at San Francisco, in the Bay Area. A brother who loves the Lord bought him an airplane ticket and sent him to Los Angeles. I went to the airport to meet and receive him to my home. During his visit, I asked him how many Gods there are. He clearly and definitely said that there are three Gods. He even went further to argue that in Psalms there are references to "gods" (82:1, 6; 138:1). I said that, by reading the context, we can know that *gods* in Psalms refers to angels. Therefore, I advised him not to say that there are three Gods, for that would be a great heresy. Please remember, today's preachers and pastors preach that there is only one true God, who is three yet one; however, in their subconscious understanding there are three Gods. According to their concept, if there were not three Gods, how could it be that the Son was standing in the water at His baptism, the Father was speaking from the heavens, and still another One was in the air? They simply cannot comprehend this in their mind.

In 1935 in Shanghai, we were discussing whether we should receive a certain famous Chinese traveling preacher to the Lord's table if he were to come in our midst. We had such a discussion because he believed that the Father, the Son, and the Spirit are three separate Gods. This is to show you that we have never been negligent in this matter. The early church fathers studied this matter in depth and with great accuracy. Concerning this matter, the creeds are very careful in their use of expressions. Although they repeatedly refer to the fact that in the Godhead there are the Father, the Son, and the Spirit, they still stress that there is only one God. Nevertheless, most preachers follow the teaching of the Eastern Orthodox Church; their teaching of the Trinity is actually tritheism.

Christ, the Son, is the mystery, the history, of God in totality. The totality of God, including not only His person but also all that pertains to Him (all the fullness of the Godhead), is in Christ. All the fullness of the Godhead refers to all that the entire God—the Father, the Son, and the Spirit—is, has, does, knows, has done, has obtained, has accomplished, and has attained; all this fullness dwells in the Son bodily. Therefore, He is truly the all-inclusive One. It is not too much to say that He is the Father because the Father is included in Him. And it is not wrong to say that He is the Spirit because the

Spirit is implied in Him. However, we absolutely confess that the Father is the Father, the Son is the Son, and the Spirit is the Spirit and that the three are distinct but not separate. In the previous chapter we pointed out that the Son is the image of the Father (Heb. 1:3; Col. 1:15a; 2 Cor. 4:4) and that the Spirit is the eyes of the Son (Zech. 3:9; 4:10; Rev. 5:6). The image of a person and the person himself are distinct but not separate; the eyes and the face are distinct but not separate. This is the mystery of the Divine Trinity.

Zechariah 3:9 says that upon one stone are seven eyes; then 4:10 says that the seven eyes are the eyes of Jehovah running to and fro on the whole earth. Revelation 5:6 says that the Lamb has seven horns and seven eyes and that the seven eyes are the seven Spirits of God. In Zechariah it is a stone, but in Revelation the stone becomes the Lamb. Furthermore, the seven eyes are the seven Spirits. We must realize that there are no new things in Revelation. Every item that is mentioned in Revelation can be found in the Old Testament. That the seven Spirits are seven eyes is referred to in Zechariah chapters three and four, but the speaking there is not clear and has to be complemented by Revelation. Likewise, the stone in Zechariah becomes the Lamb in Revelation. The stone is for building, whereas the Lamb is for redemption. This means that to accomplish God's building there must first be redemption. Hence, the stone must be the Lamb. These two are one; they both typify Christ, the Son. For this reason, I coined a new expression: "Stone-Lamb." The stone and the Lamb are just one because both have seven eyes; furthermore, these seven eyes are the seven Spirits of God. This means that the Spirit is the eyes of both the Son and the Father, who are not two or three but one.

b. He Comes in the Name of the Father and Works Also in the Name of the Father

The Son comes in the name of the Father and works also in the name of the Father. In John 5:43 the Lord said, "I have come in the name of My Father." In 10:25 He said, "The works which I do in My Father's name, these testify concerning Me." The rendering in the Mandarin Union Version implies that the Lord comes by being sent. Actually, the Lord comes not only by being sent by the Father. Rather, He comes in the name of the Father; that is, He comes with the Father. Moreover, He is in the Father's name not only in the three and a half years of His work and ministry for God; but even in the thirty-three and a half years of His human living on earth He is in the Father's name.

What does it mean that the Son comes in the name of the Father and that the Son works in the name of the Father? Let me use an example. A certain wife has a husband who has an account in the bank. When she goes to the bank to withdraw money, she does it in her husband's name. Therefore, when giving her the money, the bank teller would call out her husband's name. This means that she is in her husband's name; she and her husband are one. This example is not adequate, but there is a similarity in meaning. What the Bible means is that when the Son comes in the name of the Father, that is the Father coming, and when the Son works in the name of the Father, that is the Father working. It is true that He is the Son, but this Son is the image of the Father. Therefore, when people see Him, they see the Father. This is why when Philip said, "Lord, show us the Father," the Lord Jesus was surprised and said, "Have I been so long a time with you, and you have not known Me, Philip? He who has seen Me has seen the Father; how is it that you say, Show us the Father?" (John 14:8-9). This is truly a mystery.

c. His Name Is Called the Eternal Father

Isaiah 9:6 says, "A son is given to us;... / And His name will be called... / Eternal Father." This verse implicitly tells us that the name of the Son would be called the Eternal Father; hence, the Son and the Father are one. Although He is the Son who came in time, He is the Father in eternity.

d. He Is the Image of God to Declare God

Colossians 1:15a says, "Who [the Son of God's love] is the image of the invisible God." That the Son is the image of God means that the Son is the expression of God's being in all His attributes and virtues. This is also what John 1:18 says: "No one has ever seen God; the only begotten Son, who is in the bosom of the Father, He has declared Him." When people see the Son, they see the Father; the Son and the Father are one (10:30).

e. In His Name the Father Sends the Holy Spirit, and in His Name Also the Holy Spirit Comes

John 14:26 says, "The Comforter, the Holy Spirit, whom the Father will send in My name." The Comforter, the Holy Spirit, would be sent by the Father in the Son's name. First, the Son lives and does the works in the Father's name; then the Father sends the Holy Spirit in the Son's name. Here it says that the Father sends the Holy Spirit, but actually it is the Son who sends the Holy Spirit. Because the Father sends the Holy Spirit in the Son's name, the Father's sending is the Son's sending; the Father and the Son are one (10:30). Furthermore, since the Holy Spirit is sent in the Son's name, the Holy Spirit's coming is the Son's coming; the Holy Spirit and the Son are one (2 Cor. 3:17). This is to say that the Father sends the Holy Spirit in the Son's name and that the Holy Spirit comes also in the Son's name.

f. He Sends the Holy Spirit from and with the Father, and the Holy Spirit Also Comes from and with the Father

John 15:26 says, "But when the Comforter comes, whom I will send to you from the Father, the Spirit of reality, who proceeds from the Father." John 14:26 says that the Father sends the Holy Spirit in the Son's name and that the Holy Spirit comes in the Son's name. Yet in 15:26 it says that the Son sends the Holy Spirit from the Father and that this Spirit proceeds from the Father. This means that the Father is the Son because the Father is in the Son's name. Not only so, the Greek word for *from* in 15:26 is *para,* which means "from with." This means that the Son sends the Holy Spirit from and with the Father; moreover, the Holy Spirit also comes from and with the Father. Therefore, these two verses show us that the Divine Trinity is actually the One who is three yet one.

The dispute between the Catholic Church and the Eastern Orthodox Church is in these two verses; this is also the reason that the original church was divided into two. The Eastern Orthodox Church believes that the Spirit proceeds only from the Father and that only the Father is the source of the Spirit. The Catholic Church believes that both the Father and the Son are the source and that the Spirit comes from both the Father and the Son as the source. Actually, the Holy Spirit comes from the Father, who is in the name of the Son. Therefore, to come from the Son is to come from the Father, and to come from the Father is to come from the Son. Furthermore, when the Holy Spirit comes from the Father and the Son as the source, He does not leave the source but He comes with the source. When we put these two verses together, we discover that the Holy Spirit is sent by the Father in the Son's name and that He comes with the Father. The Holy Spirit is also sent by the Son from and with the Father. Therefore, the Holy Spirit comes not only from and with the Father but also through and with the Son. Eventually, who is it that comes? It is the Triune God who comes; that is, the Father, the Son, and the Spirit all come together.

The whole matter lies with the word *send*. The Father's sending is the Son's sending; the Father and the Son are one. When the Holy Spirit is sent, He comes with the Son in the Son's name and He comes also from and with the Father. Hence, when the Holy Spirit reaches us, the whole Triune God comes. Concerning the Triune God, sometimes you feel that He nourishes and cherishes you as the Son, while other times you feel that He disciplines and gives grace to you as the Father; but most of the time you sense that He is interceding for you as the Spirit. This is the Triune God—the Father, the Son, and the Spirit—reaching man consummately as the Spirit.

I was with the Brethren when I was young. They taught us that when we pray we can pray only to the heavenly Father, in the Son's name, and by the power of the Holy Spirit, without any confusion. However, when I prayed, I often made mistakes and therefore had to confess and repent of my sin. This shows that the teaching concerning the Divine Trinity greatly affects our Christian life. Later, when I studied these two verses, I found out the story about the sending of the Holy Spirit by the Father, the Son, and the Spirit. The Father's sending in the Son's name is the Son's sending from the Father. Furthermore, the One who is sent comes from and with the Father, and He comes also with the Son in the Son's name. Eventually, all three of Them come. Today's Christian teachers mostly teach tritheism, saying that when the Son comes, He comes alone, leaving the Father in heaven. Most of them have neither the knowledge nor the experience concerning the Spirit. Yet we have seen this matter in the holy Word of God, and we can also experience it subjectively.

g. He Is the Spirit

In 2 Corinthians 3:17 Paul abruptly said that "the Lord is the Spirit." Today, our critics are most afraid of three Scripture verses: 1 Corinthians 15:45; 2 Corinthians 3:17; and Isaiah 9:6. First Corinthians 15:45 says, "The last Adam became a life-giving Spirit." Some say that the Spirit in this verse is not the Holy Spirit; instead, they say that this verse speaks of Christ becoming a Spirit. However, the Spirit here is modified by *life-giving,* indicating that this Spirit is the Holy Spirit, because in the universe there is no other Spirit who gives life besides the Holy Spirit.

Some say that "the Lord" in 2 Corinthians 3:17 is a general title of God and that it does not denote the Lord Jesus. However, according to the context, "the Lord" here should refer to Christ the Lord. Verses 14 and 16 of chapter three say, "The veil is being done away with in Christ....But whenever their heart turns to the Lord, the veil is taken away." Verse 17 continues to say, "And the Lord is the Spirit." Then in 4:5 Paul said, "For we do not preach ourselves but Christ Jesus as Lord." Obviously, the Lord here refers to Christ the Lord. Paul said that this Lord is the Spirit.

Furthermore, Isaiah 9:6 says, "A son is given to us;... / And His name will be called... / Eternal Father." Some say that the Father here does not refer to the heavenly Father but to a Father of eternity. They say that *eternal* (an adjective) should be properly rendered *eternity* (a noun), just like saying that George Washington is the father of America and Thomas Edison is the father of electricity. However, the writer wrote this verse in the form of a couplet with "child" and "Mighty God" as a pair and with "son" and "Eternal Father" as another pair. The child is the son, and God is the Father. Since there is only one God, there is surely also only one Father. No one can twist this word and say that the Father here does not refer to the Father in the Godhead but to another Father. Furthermore, we must interpret any verse of the Bible according to the particular book in which the verse is found. In the entire book of Isaiah, Jehovah is referred to twice as our Father (63:16; 64:8), indicating that the Eternal Father refers to God, who is our Father. Therefore, we cannot say that He is the Eternal Father and not our Father.

The Son as the Spirit is the embodiment of the Triune God. After completing all the processes, such as incarnation, human living, crucifixion, resurrection, ascension, and glorification, He became "the Spirit" (John 7:39; Rom. 8:26-27; Gal. 3:2, 14) as the ultimate manifestation of the Triune God.

h. He Is the One Who Fills All in All

The Son is also the One who fills all in all. Ephesians 1:22-23 says, "The church, which is His Body, the fullness of the One who fills all in all." That the church is the Body, the fullness, of Christ means that through the enjoyment of the riches of Christ the church becomes the fullness of Christ for His expression. This Christ as the infinite God is not limited by anything. He is so great that He fills all in all. *All* includes being so extensive that it is beyond our imagination. In His divinity, Christ is the unlimited One.

2. In His Humanity

a. He Became Flesh, Partaking of Blood and Flesh and Taking the Likeness of the Flesh of Sin

Hebrews 2:14 says, "Since therefore the children have shared in blood and flesh, He also Himself in like manner partook of the same." John 1:14 says that "the Word became flesh." First John 4:2 says that "Jesus Christ has come in the flesh." These three verses tell us clearly that in His humanity Christ became flesh, partaking of blood and flesh. His body of blood and flesh is a real body; it is not merely a phantasm, as taught by the Docetists.

The body of blood and flesh is not a good entity; it is the flesh of sin. However, according to Romans 8:3 the Lord Jesus did not become the flesh of sin itself; rather, He became a man of flesh "in the likeness of the flesh of sin." This matter is typified by the bronze serpent (Num. 21:9). John 3:14 says, "And as Moses lifted up the serpent in the wilderness, so must the Son of Man be lifted up." The Lord Jesus was lifted up like the bronze serpent, which had the form, the shape, of the serpent but was without the serpent's poison, the serpent's nature. Furthermore, the bronze serpent is joined to Satan, just as the likeness of the flesh of sin is joined to the fallen man. However, the Lord only had the form but not the real substance, the poison. Hence, when He was put to death on the cross, in God's eyes, Satan was there and a sinner was there. This is what Hebrews 2:14 says: "He...Himself in like manner partook of the same [blood and flesh], that through death He might destroy him who has the might of death, that is, the devil." This means that, because the devil is in the flesh, when the Lord dealt with the flesh on the cross, He also dealt with and destroyed Satan, who belongs to the flesh. How could the Lord destroy Satan by becoming the flesh? The reason is that the flesh is involved with Satan—Satan is in the flesh of the fallen man and is the poison in the flesh of man.

b. He Became a Man

First Timothy 2:5 says, "For there is one God and one Mediator of God and men, the man Christ Jesus." The Lord Jesus was God from eternity (John 1:1). In time He became a man through incarnation (v. 14). While He was living on earth, He was a man and He was also God (1 Tim. 3:16). After His resurrection He is still a man (Acts 7:56) and also God (John 20:28).

Philippians 2:6-8 says that He, existing in the form of God, emptied Himself, taking the form of a slave, becoming in the

likeness of men, and being found in fashion as a man. When
the Lord Jesus became a man, He became a bona fide man.
He humbled Himself, lowering His status from that of God to
that of a man. He had the likeness of a man, the outward
appearance of humanity. He was also found in fashion as a
man, having the outward guise, the semblance, of humanity.
He humbled Himself even to the extent that, instead of being
a high-class person, He became a slave to serve people (Mark
10:45). There is only one thing that was in man but not in
Him, and that thing is sin. He did not have the poison of sin
that is in man; in Him Satan has nothing (John 14:30).
Although the creeds mention that the Lord Jesus was incarnated to become a man, even a perfect man, Christianity does
not have much appreciation of the Lord Jesus' taking the
form of a slave, becoming in the likeness of men, and being
found in fashion as a man. In the Lord's recovery we should
treasure and appreciate this matter.

c. He Is the Firstborn of All Creation

Christ is all-inclusive; He includes both God and man.
Since He includes God, in the Divine Trinity He is not only
the Son, but He is also called the Father, and He is also the
Spirit. Since He includes man, He became flesh as a man,
taking the form of a slave, having the likeness of men, and
being found in fashion as a man. Furthermore, He includes
all creation and is the Firstborn of all creation. For this
reason, the inclusiveness of Christ is complete.

Angels are part of the creation; hence, the Lord Jesus
also includes the angels. He is the Angel of Jehovah (Exo.
3:2-15; 14:19; 23:20-21; Judg. 13:15-21). In Revelation, He is
the "another Angel" who takes care of God's people on earth
(7:2-3), adds His fragrance to the prayers of the saints and
offers them before God (8:3), treads on the sea and on the land
to take possession of the whole earth (10:1-2), and destroys
Babylon the Great (18:1-2). The Lord Jesus even includes
fallen men because He Himself became flesh. Romans and
Galatians reveal clearly that the flesh denotes fallen man
(Rom. 3:20; Gal. 2:16). Therefore, He is all-inclusive; He is not
only the Creator but also a creature.

Christ includes man. Furthermore, He became a man with flesh, having human blood, flesh, and bones. At His crucifixion, not one of His bones was broken (John 19:33-36). Blood, flesh, and bones evidently belong to a created being; therefore, it is illogical to say that the Lord Jesus is not a creature. Since Christ partook of blood and flesh (Heb. 2:14), having a body with human blood, flesh, and bones, how could He not be a created One? As God, Christ is the Creator; as a man, Christ is a creature. In His divinity, He is the Creator; in His humanity, since He became flesh, His flesh was something created. Hence, we must confess that He is the Creator and also a creature. To say that the Lord Jesus is not a creature is equivalent to denying that He has come in the flesh; such denial was a heresy strongly condemned by the apostle John (1 John 4:2-3).

Since Christ is a creature in His humanity, when was He created? Arius asserted that since Christ is a creature, He is not the eternal God, but He was created by God at a certain period in eternity as the first created One. Hence, in this thought, there was a time when Christ did not exist. This is a great heresy. Colossians 1:15b says that Christ is "the First-born of all creation." This means that, in God's eternal plan, in God's eternal economy, the Triune God agreed that the Son would become a man, would become flesh. From that time on, in the eyes of God, the Son has been a creature. Then, in time, He actually came to be a man.

Some may ask, "It was two thousand years ago when the Lord Jesus became a man in time, and before that time there were already millions and millions of people; how can we say that He is the Firstborn of all creation?" We have already said that God's calculation is different from man's calculation. For example, Adam is the first man created by God, so the second man should be Cain. Yet the Bible says that the second man is Christ (1 Cor. 15:47). Furthermore, since the first Adam is the beginning of mankind, all human beings are descendants of Adam and all of them are "Adams." Thus, there are Adams being born every day; so the last Adam should have not come yet. However, the Bible says that Christ is not only the second man but also the last Adam (v. 45). This is God's calculation.

Furthermore, according to history the Lord Jesus was crucified two thousand years ago. According to Scripture, however, He is the Lamb who was slain from the foundation of the world (Rev. 13:8). Long before Christ was born, He was slain from the foundation of the world; this is God's estimation. Hence, we cannot consider the all-inclusiveness of Christ according to our view. In Genesis 18, as early as the time of Abraham, Christ appeared to Abraham in the form of a man with a real body, and His feet were washed and He ate the meal that Abraham prepared. According to man's view, how could Christ appear as a man before His incarnation? In Judges 13, as the Angel of Jehovah, Christ appeared as a man to Manoah and his wife (vv. 10-11). Manoah asked the Angel of Jehovah for His name, and He said, "Why do you ask about My name, since it is wonderful?" (vv. 17-18). His name is wonderful because He is the Angel of Jehovah and He is also Jehovah, yet He appeared as a man. This is truly beyond human understanding. Therefore, instead of trying to comprehend these truths with our minds, we should simply receive them by faith according to God's revelation.

d. He Is the Firstborn from the Dead

Colossians 1:18 says that Christ is "the Head of the Body, the church; He is the beginning, the Firstborn from the dead." This means that Christ is the first in resurrection; as the Head of the Body, He occupies the first place in the church. God has two creations: one is the old creation, which refers to the creation of the universe; the other is the new creation, which refers to the bringing forth of the church (2 Cor. 5:17; Eph. 2:15). Christ is not only the Firstborn of the old creation but also the Firstborn of the new creation.

e. He Became the Life-giving Spirit in Resurrection

First Corinthians 15:45 says, "The last Adam became a life-giving Spirit." The last Adam is Christ. In incarnation He became flesh for redemption (John 1:14, 29); then in resurrection He was transfigured and became a life-giving Spirit for the imparting of life (10:10b). Christ has to be such a Spirit that He may impart life to man. In the evening of the day of His resurrection, when He came into the midst of the disciples and breathed into them that they might receive the Holy Spirit (20:19-22), He breathed Himself into them as the life-giving Spirit, thereby imparting Himself into them as their life and everything.

f. The Spirit of God Became His Spirit, the Spirit of Jesus Christ

At the beginning of the New Testament, the Spirit of God is the Holy Spirit (Matt. 1:18, 20; Luke 1:35). After the resurrection of the Lord, the Spirit of God became "the Spirit" (John 7:39), the life-giving Spirit. This Spirit is also the Spirit of Jesus Christ. Hence, Acts 16:7 mentions "the Spirit of Jesus," Romans 8:9 mentions "the Spirit of Christ," and Philippians 1:19 mentions "the Spirit of Jesus Christ." The Spirit of Jesus is mainly related to the Lord's humanity and human living; the Spirit of Christ is mainly related to the Lord's resurrection; the Spirit of Jesus Christ is the Spirit of God compounded with the Lord's incarnation, human living, crucifixion, and resurrection. This compound Spirit is typified by the holy anointing ointment in Exodus 30:23-25, a compound of olive oil and four kinds of spices. How could the Spirit of God become the Spirit of Jesus, the Spirit of Christ, and the Spirit of Jesus Christ? It was accomplished through His incarnation, human living, death, and resurrection.

g. He Poured Out the Holy Spirit Whom He Had Received from the Father, and He Gives the Spirit Not by Measure

Furthermore, the Lord Jesus poured out the Holy Spirit whom He had received from the Father, and He gives the Spirit not by measure. Acts 2:33 says, "Therefore having been exalted to the right hand of God and having received the promise of the Holy Spirit from the Father, He has poured out this which you both see and hear." The exalted Christ's receiving of the promise of the Holy Spirit was actually His receiving of the Holy Spirit Himself. Christ was conceived of the Holy Spirit essentially for His existence in humanity (Luke 1:35; Matt. 1:18, 20) and was anointed with the Spirit economically for His ministry among men (Matt. 3:16; Luke 4:18). After His resurrection and ascension, He needed to receive the Spirit economically again that He might pour Himself out upon His Body to carry out His heavenly ministry on earth for the accomplishing of God's New Testament economy.

John 3:34 says that Christ "gives the Spirit not by measure." This shows that the Son dispenses the Spirit to the believers without measure. As the Head of the church, Christ not only pours out the Holy Spirit but also dispenses the Spirit to the believers without measure.

The creeds were written in such a simple way that all these crucial points were omitted. I believe that some of those who formulated the creeds saw these points but, since they were not able to explain them thoroughly, they did not dare to speak about them. How do you explain the fact that the Lord is the Spirit? How do you explain the fact that the Son is called the Father? The more you say, the more mistakes you make; therefore, it is better not to say anything. It is probably because of this that they wrote in a very concise way. Consequently, those who later read the creeds suffered a great loss. Our burden is to find out all the crucial points.

h. He Was Begotten with His Humanity in Resurrection to Be the Firstborn Son of God with Many Brothers

Christ was begotten with His humanity in resurrection to be the firstborn Son of God with many brothers. Is not the Lord Jesus the only begotten Son of God? Why then is He also the firstborn Son of God? How can this be? If you ask Christian teachers, you can hardly find one who is able to answer these questions. Most likely they will tell you not to be too particular about this matter and that nevertheless He is the Son of God. I asked my pastor about this when I was young. He said, "Don't ask anymore; your head is too big. Anyway, it is too hard to explain what is meant by the firstborn Son of God and the only begotten Son of God."

Actually, the light in the Scriptures concerning this matter is very clear. Quoting from Psalm 2, Acts 13:33 says,

"You are My Son; this day have I begotten You." *Begotten* here does not refer to the birth of the Lord Jesus in the manger; rather, it refers to His birth when He came out of the tomb, the birth of the man Jesus when He was raised up by God. By death and resurrection, the humanity which the man Jesus had put on was uplifted into divinity. When His humanity entered divinity, He became the Son of God also in His humanity. This is to be "sonized." Before His resurrection Christ was the Son of God only in His divinity; in His humanity He was not yet the Son of God but was the Son of Man. However, through His resurrection His humanity was brought into divinity; thus, He was begotten to be the Son of God in His humanity. Therefore, after His resurrection His being the Son of God was a different situation. In His divinity He was the only begotten Son of God from eternity past (John 1:18; 3:16), but in His humanity He became the firstborn Son of God through resurrection (Rom. 8:29; Heb. 1:6).

As the Son of God in His divinity, He is uniquely one; but after He was begotten as the Son of God in resurrection with His humanity, He is not uniquely one. In His resurrection He regenerated all His believers (1 Pet. 1:3) as His many brothers and as the many sons of God. Therefore, Romans 8:29 says that the Lord Jesus is the Firstborn among many brothers. John 20:17 tells us that in the morning of His resurrection the Lord said to Mary, "Go to My brothers and say to them, I ascend to My Father and your Father, and My God and your God." Prior to that morning, He did not have brothers, but now His brothers were born with Him at the same time. Then, Hebrews 2:11-12 tells us that after His resurrection the Lord came into the midst of the disciples and declared the Father's name to His brothers. At this time His brothers had become the church, in the midst of which He came to praise the Father's name.

i. He Was Made Both Lord and Christ
in Ascension

In His humanity Christ was made both Lord and Christ in ascension. Acts 2:36 says that after His resurrection and ascension Christ was made both Lord and Christ. As God, the

Lord was the Lord all the time (Luke 1:43; John 11:21; 20:28). But as man, He was made the Lord in His ascension after He brought His humanity into divinity in His resurrection. As God's sent and anointed One, He was Christ from the time that He was born (Matt. 1:16; Luke 2:11; Matt. 16:16). But as such a One, He was also officially made the very Christ of God in His ascension.

As God, Christ was the Lord from eternity. Then by incarnation He became Jesus, a Nazarene. This man was neither the Lord nor the Son of God in His humanity. But when He entered into resurrection, this man became the Son of God, and in His ascension this man was made the Lord. Before His resurrection, in His divinity He was the Lord from eternity. But after His ascension, He was made the Lord in His humanity. Thus, He is the Lord both in His divinity and in His humanity. Therefore, today there is a Man in heaven who is the Lord of all. In the same principle, He was also made Christ. He was made Lord, the Lord of all (Acts 10:36), to possess all; He was also made Christ, God's Anointed (Heb. 1:9), to carry out God's commission.

j. He Is the Heir of All Things

Hebrews 1:2 says that God has appointed the Son to be the Heir of all things. We know that, at the beginning of Hebrews 1, verses 2 and 3 unfold to us both the person and work of the Son. In His person He is the effulgence of God's glory and the impress of God's substance. In His work He created the universe and upholds and bears all things; He also made purification of our sins and accomplished redemption. Now He is sitting down on the right hand of God until His enemies become a footstool for His feet.

In the past He was the Creator of all things (Heb. 1:2, 10; John 1:3; Col. 1:16; 1 Cor. 8:6); in the present He is the Upholder of all things and the One who bears all things (Heb. 1:3); in the future He will be the Heir who inherits all things. All things belong to Him, are for Him, and will be inherited by Him. Therefore, Romans 11:36 says, "Out from Him and through Him and to Him are all things."

A CONCLUDING WORD

We must very clearly see the divinity and humanity of Christ to be able to understand the mystery of the Divine Trinity. In conclusion, God is three, having three persons—the Father, the Son, and the Spirit—yet He is surely one, being the one God. When we receive any one of the three, we receive all of Them. When we have the Son, we also have the Father and the Spirit; when we have the Spirit, we also have the Father and the Son. Therefore, when the Spirit comes, the consummation of the Father, the Son, and the Spirit comes; the all-inclusive Spirit comes. As such a Spirit, Christ fills all and includes all. And as the Spirit, Christ comes into us to be our enjoyment.

Here I would like to refer to two hymns. The first one is *Hymns,* #113, a hymn on praising the Lord as our Redeemer. The climax of this hymn is in stanza 5:

> Though angels praise the heavenly King,
> And worship Him as God alone,
> We can with exultation sing,
> "He wears our nature on the throne."

Another hymn is #132, which is also on praising the Lord for His humanity. This hymn is full of life, full of the Spirit, and full of experience. Stanza 1 says,

> Lo! in heaven Jesus sitting,
>   Christ the Lord is there enthroned;
> As the man by God exalted,
>   With God's glory He is crowned.

Then stanzas 4 through 6 deal with life, the Spirit, and experience:

> He as God with man is mingled,
>   God in man is testified;
> He as man with God is blended,
>   Man in God is glorified.

> From the Glorified in heaven
>   The inclusive Spirit came;
> All of Jesus' work and Person
>   Doth this Spirit here proclaim.

> With the Glorified in heaven
> Is the Church identified;
> By the Spirit of this Jesus
> Are His members edified.

The hymn reaches its climax in stanza 7:

> Lo! a man is now in heaven
> As the Lord of all enthroned;
> This is Jesus Christ our Savior,
> With God's glory ever crowned!

Nearly none of the eighteen points which we have mentioned above was written as a hymn. There are over ten thousand hymns in Christianity, but they do not cover these points. Instead, most of them are concerning God's compassion, God's holiness, God's righteousness, God's power, and even superficial items such as miracles and wonders. Yes, the creeds mention Christ's being born as a man to save sinners. If we carefully study the New Testament, we will see that Christ became flesh not only to save sinners but, even more, to carry out God's eternal economy, which is to work God into men that they may become children of God to be the Body of Christ for the expression of the Triune God in eternity. This is the highest goal of God's becoming flesh.

Most of the matters preached in Christianity today are very shallow. We do not deny that the things preached are right, that Christ became flesh to die and shed His blood to save sinners; this, however, is not the ultimate purpose. The ultimate goal of God's becoming flesh is to dispense Himself into man that man may be one with Him in life and nature and be joined and mingled with Him as one to be His corporate expression. This is our commission today in the Lord's recovery. Therefore, when we lead you to go out to knock on doors, we do not preach the low gospel but preach the meaning of human life instead. The meaning of human life is that man needs to have God within him. This includes God's becoming flesh and passing through death and resurrection before He can come into man. Of course, because man is sinful, He had to make redemption for man; this is right. But redemption is not the goal; it is the procedure for reaching the goal, and the goal is that God wants to enter into man to dispense Himself as man's life and nature that man may be joined to Him to be a part of His organism for His corporate expression. This is what we must see and practice.

This is the gospel. I hope that this is what you preach when you go out to preach the gospel. Do not think that people cannot understand; they surely can understand. I often say that actually it is not that people cannot understand, but rather it is that you yourself do not understand and therefore you do not know how to preach, and you cannot preach. I hope that you will all rise up to speak the high gospel, preach the great word, and announce the eternal mystery. You need to preach this as the gospel.

Furthermore, I also hope that the young people will rise up and learn to write hymns with all the above crucial items. For many years I have been wanting to re-compile our hymnal, because some of the hymns are truly not suitable and we do not sing them anymore. The melody and poetry of *Hymns,* #113 are very good but most of the content is too low; therefore, we rarely sing it. I hope that this kind of hymn would be eliminated and replaced by hymns of higher quality. In the compilation of the hymnal, my understanding is that Brother Nee's selection was based on three points: first, general Christian hymns on the knowledge of God; second, hymns by the inner life people on the experience of the cross and the growth in life; and third, hymns by the Brethren with words of praise. In 1960 I felt that there was a great lack in our hymnal concerning the Spirit and the riches in life as well as concerning Christ and the church. Therefore, I wrote over eighty hymns within two months, most of which are on the Spirit, life, Christ, and the church. Then when I was compiling the English hymnal twenty-five years ago in America, I added nearly two hundred more hymns in these categories. Due to lack of time, however, I did not include the crucial items mentioned above. I hope that the young people will gradually rise up and make an effort to learn how to write hymns and to compile a new hymnal.

I am very happy that in the last ten years, and in particular the last five years, wherever I went to attend the Lord's table meeting, I observed that the brothers and sisters' understanding has been uplifted. Most of the hymns they sang are concerning God's dispensing Himself into us, Christ as our life, and the church as His expression. Fifty years ago our favorite hymn was: "How pleasant is the sound of praise! / It well becomes the saints of God; / Should we refuse our songs to raise, / The stones might tell our shame abroad" (*Hymns,* #113). But now we do not select it any longer because its content is low. If I were to show you the hymns that I wrote sixty years ago, you would all feel that they are shallow. However, with my growth in life and my increase in the knowledge of the spiritual truths, hymns that are crystals came out. Poems and songs are the crystallization of our learning and our knowledge of God. I hope that you will learn more and be more equipped, especially concerning the eighteen points covered in this chapter. Then gradually you will be able to write some hymns of high quality. This is a need in the Lord's recovery.

CHAPTER FIVE

THE ECONOMY OF GOD

Scripture Reading: Eph. 1:9-11; 3:9-11; 1 Tim. 1:3-4; Eph. 1:5; Rom. 8:3; Gal. 4:4, 6; John 3:6; 4:24; Rom. 8:16, 14; John 17:2; 2 Pet. 1:4; Eph. 2:19; John 14:2; 1 Cor. 1:30; Acts 2:38; Matt. 28:19b; Rom. 6:3b, 4a; Eph. 2:5-6; John 20:22; Acts 1:8a; Rom. 11:17-24; 1 Cor. 12:12; Eph. 5:30; 1:22-23; 2:15; Rev. 1:11; Acts 26:18; Heb. 2:11; 1 Pet. 1:3a; Rom. 9:21; Eph. 5:27; 1 Pet. 2:5

OUTLINE

II. The second item of the vision—the economy of God:
   A. Being His household administration, dispensation, and plan.
   B. To work Himself, in His Divine Trinity, into His chosen ones.
   C. That they may become His children as His sons with His life and nature to become His house so that He may have a dwelling place for His rest.
   D. That they may have an organic union with the Divine Trinity in Christ to become the members of Christ that constitute His Body as the corporate expression of the Triune God in Christ.

STUDYING TO UNDERSTAND THE TRUTH
CONCERNING THE DIVINE TRINITY

In the previous chapters we saw the revelation concerning the Divine Trinity. In order to understand the matter of the Trinity, on the negative side, we must see the fifteen shortages of the creeds. The Bible has no shortage; rather, it is full in contents. The creeds, however, are very inadequate. This is why after the formulation of the creeds, people throughout the ages were always adding items to them. However, despite the additions, the creeds are still inadequate. I hope that you would exert much effort to study, enter into, understand, and remember the fifteen items which I listed so that you may be able to apply them when the occasion arises. This is an assignment for you.

On the positive side, we also need to see the all-inclusiveness of Christ. Colossians 2:16-17 says, "In eating and in drinking or in respect of a feast or of a new moon or of the Sabbath, which are a shadow of the things to come, but the body is of Christ." Food, drink, feast, new moon, and Sabbath are not persons but things, which are just shadows; but the real body is Christ. This means that Christ is our real food, real drink, real feast, real new moon, and real Sabbath. Furthermore, Ephesians 1:22-23 says, "The church, which is His Body, the fullness of the One who fills all in all." This indicates that Christ is so inclusive that no human words can describe Him in full; He is all-inclusive.

More than twenty years ago when I first went to America to speak about these truths, there were opposers who slandered me, accusing me of being a pantheist. They said that I am from the Far East, where most of the people believe in pantheism. This really shows the ignorance of the opposing ones. If they had truly been enlightened, they would be able to see that the Lord Jesus is One who is so inclusive, extensive, and unlimited.

Some theologians, failing to see the inclusiveness of Christ, are just like the blind feeling the elephant, touching only a particular part. Yet they would cling to it, engage in unending arguments about it, and use it to condemn others. This is exactly what happened to me in America. On the one hand, they rely too much on the creeds as a basis, not realizing that the creeds are short in many aspects and therefore are not qualified to serve as a standard or basis. On the other hand, they lack the view of Christ's inclusiveness and therefore become very shallow and shortsighted. For example, based on Colossians 1:15b we say that Christ is the Firstborn of all creation. Our critics then say that we teach Arianism. Yet they have not seen that Christ is not only a creature but also the Firstborn of all creatures—He is the man among all men. The Bible does not speak about Christ's being a man in a brief and simple way. Rather, it says that Christ was a man in form, in likeness, and in fashion and that He also was in the likeness of the flesh of sin. All these descriptions are very particular.

In the past few years a certain theologian published a study Bible based on the King James Version. For John 1:14, he wrote a note on "the Word was made flesh," saying that the Lord Jesus joined Himself to sinless humanity in His incarnation. This is because the general human concept is that when the Lord Jesus became flesh, it could not be that He became a flesh of sin. However, since the author of that study Bible is a Doctor of Divinity, after carefully studying the context, he must have felt that his statement had no standing ground. Therefore, in the revised edition he said that the Lord Jesus joined Himself to sinful humanity in His incarnation. Hence, if theologians hastily decide on doctrinal matters without a full view of Christ's all-inclusiveness, they will make big mistakes.

According to the type or figure, the Lord Jesus died on the cross in the likeness of the flesh of sin. When He was crucified, on the one hand, He was in the form of a lamb because He was the Lamb of God (1:29); on the other hand, He was in the form of the bronze serpent, having the form of the serpent but without the serpent's poison. He said that as Moses lifted up the serpent in the wilderness, so He, the Son of Man in the flesh, would be lifted up (3:14). This means that He Himself acknowledged and implicitly told us that the bronze serpent in the Old Testament was a type, a figure, of Himself. In the Bible, records such as these are too numerous to recount.

In Revelation 5, the apostle John wept much when he saw that no one in the universe was able to open the mystery of God's economy. Then one of the angels said to him, "Do not weep; behold, the Lion of the tribe of Judah, the Root of David, has overcome so that He may open the scroll and its seven seals." What the angel introduced was a Lion, yet what John saw was a Lamb (vv. 1-7). Is Christ a Lion or a Lamb? We can only say that He is a Lion-Lamb. Christ is not only a Lion-Lamb but also a Stone-Lamb. This is based upon the fact that in Revelation the Lamb has seven eyes, yet in Zechariah chapters three and four the seven eyes are upon a stone. From these verses we can see that the Lord Jesus is not so simple.

I am giving you these illustrations to let you know that to understand the truth concerning the Divine Trinity you need to see the inadequacy of the creeds and the inclusiveness of Christ. There are two major items with eighteen points concerning Christ's inclusiveness. The major items are His divinity and His humanity. If you study these two aspects thoroughly, you will be able not only to avoid theological errors but also to enter into the enjoyment of the riches of Christ. You will be able to see and experience that Christ is the Triune God. He is the Father, the Son, and the Spirit, yet He is three-one. He is definitely one, yet in the oneness there is still a distinction, but no separation. You can say that the Father is distinct from the Son, the Son is distinct from the Spirit, and the Spirit is distinct from the Father and the Son. Their distinctions, however, are in oneness. This is where the mystery lies. Once your eyes are enlightened to know the inclusiveness of Christ, only then can you see that the three in the divine Godhead are distinct, yet They are always one. They are one God, not three Gods.

We can say that the all-inclusive Christ is the embodiment of the Triune God. When we see Him, we see the Triune God. The Spirit is the ultimate consummation, the ultimate manifestation, of the processed Triune God. Therefore, when we have the Spirit, we have the Triune God—not just the simple Triune God, but the processed Triune God. Today the Christ whom we enjoy is such a One. When you have a real knowledge of the inclusiveness of Christ, it will help you to enjoy Him.

THE WAY TO STUDY THE TRUTH

I have recommended the book *Concerning the Person of Christ* for your reading. Although it is just a pamphlet, its discussion is comprehensive. It shows you both the wrong interpretations and the proper knowledge of men throughout the centuries concerning the Person of Christ, and it also cites numerous Scripture verses. It is truly worth your reading. The matters which it covers are not my own teachings. Rather, they are all based upon the Bible with the pertinent verses excerpted. You should read the book carefully. For example, in the Old Testament, one of the designations of the Lord Jesus is a "Shoot." As the Shoot of David (Jer. 23:5; 33:15; Zech. 3:8; 6:12), He sprouted out of David. And as the Shoot of Jehovah (Isa. 4:2), He sprouted out of God. This means that as a Shoot, Christ has two origins: one origin is David, the human origin; the other origin is God, the divine origin. All these things are in the Bible and require your painstaking study. I have already done the foundational work on these items, and they are all listed in the pamphlet *Concerning the Person of Christ*.

Your training here may be compared to graduate school. There is no need for the professor to say too much; you just need to study carefully on your own according to the reading list, and if necessary, the professor will give you a little guidance. Moreover, there is no need for you to go to a "library" far away. The "library" in our midst is very convenient. As long as you are willing to spend your time and energy, you will be able to get all these things into you. I hope that all of the young brothers and sisters who have the desire to serve the Lord full-time permanently could learn an initial outline of the truth within a short period of a few months. At least you should learn and know which books you can go to so that you can find the material you need. This does not mean that you will be fully trained after four months. You still have a long way to go, and there are too many things that you need to study. What I hope is that after four months your field of vision will be widened to know a little bit about the way and at least know where to go to find the proper materials. Hence, in these four months I am trying to lead you only to the beginning of the road. But whether or not it will be a thoroughfare leading to great success depends on how you press forward on your own. You must continue to learn more and more.

II. THE SECOND ITEM OF THE VISION— THE ECONOMY OF GOD

In this chapter we will go on to see the second item of the vision, and that is the economy of God. In the recent ten or so years we have released many messages and published a number of books concerning this matter. If you really have the heart, you should spend time to study those books. In this training the outlines that I give you will serve only as a guide that you may know which route to take in order to know the economy of God. You need to spend more time to dig and find the rest of the riches.

A. Being His Household Administration, Dispensation, and Plan

There are over three hundred passages in the Bible referring to the economy of God either directly or indirectly. In this chapter we will mention only three passages: Ephesians 1:9-11; 3:9-11; and 1 Timothy 1:3-4. What is mentioned mainly in these three portions is the matter of "economy." Ephesians 1:10 says, "Unto the economy of the fullness of the times"; Ephesians 3:9 says, "And to enlighten all that they may see what the economy of the mystery is, which throughout the ages has been hidden in God, who created all things." First Timothy 1:4 says, "God's economy, which is in faith." The Greek word for *economy* in these three passages is *oikonomia,* which means "household law"; it denotes "a household management," "a household administration," and derivatively, "a dispensation," "a plan," or "an economy for administration."

I would like to call your attention to some of the crucial vocabulary used in Ephesians 1:9-11 and 3:9-11, such as *will, good pleasure, economy* (or, *dispensation, plan*), and *eternal purpose,* which are all included in the matter pertaining to the economy of God; this indicates that what is implied in the economy of God is very rich.

The Greek word *oikonomia* is made up of two words: *oikos,* denoting a "house" or "household," and *nomos,* denoting a "law" or "principle." The meaning of these two words combined is "household administration." This house is the house of God, including all the saved ones in the whole human race, all those who were chosen by God and have received God as their life (Eph. 2:19). They are a group of people who became the new creation by receiving God's life through God's selection. They are a big family of God. Furthermore, in this big family we are the masters and all the angels are the servants who wait upon us, ministering to us as those who inherit so great a salvation (Heb. 1:14).

In this universal house, there is the need for a household administration to arrive at a specific purpose. Whenever there is a household administration, it is necessary to have a dispensation and a plan. This is not a small matter. With the household administration, there is a dispensation; with the dispensation, there is the need for a plan. Hence, when God makes His dispensation, He designs a number of administrative procedures for the carrying out of His economy. For this reason, *oikonomia* may also be rendered *dispensation,* which means "arrangement" or "plan," referring to God's plan for His administration. In God's administration, God's plan, there are many dispensations and many ways.

At the end of the last century, Bible scholars found from the Scriptures the so-called seven dispensations. Actually, these seven dispensations are not seven ages but God's seven administrative procedures. In each procedure God has a different way of dealing with man. For example, in the Old Testament age after the time of Moses, God's way of dealing with man was according to the law; hence, that was "the dispensation of law." In the New Testament age, God's administration is according to grace, and He deals with man according to grace; hence, it is called "the dispensation of grace." In the millennial kingdom, God will take the kingdom as His administration and as His way of dealing with man; hence, it is called "the dispensation of the kingdom." Therefore, the word *dispensation* does not denote an age; it denotes a plan, an arrangement, a procedure. In all the dispensations and plans there are many administrative procedures. This somewhat explains the meaning of God's economy.

B. To Work Himself, in His Divine Trinity, into His Chosen Ones

The purpose of God in His economy is to work Himself, in His Divine Trinity, into His chosen ones. This God who has a plan, an economy, wants to do only one thing, that is, to work Himself into His chosen ones through all the processes and procedures which He went through in His Divine Trinity. The entire Bible reveals that God wants to work Himself into His chosen ones by passing through various processes in His Divine Trinity.

Christians read Ephesians chapter one and accept what it says. At the outset, this chapter says that God chose us before the foundation of the world and then He predestinated us. When I was with the Brethren in my youth, I heard their proper teaching and obtained a clear knowledge as well concerning God's selection and predestination. Yet I never heard them tell me what the purpose of God's selection and predestination was. They only said that God chose us and predestinated us that we may receive an inheritance. And the inheritance which they spoke of, according to my understanding, is a heavenly blessing in the future, which may be a very pleasant dwelling place. This corresponds with the traditional concept of the Chinese, which is that the children shall receive some material things from their father as an inheritance. Thus, the impression that I had from listening to the messages in the Brethren church was that God chose us and predestinated us that we may enjoy the eternal blessing and receive an inheritance. However, they did not see that the same chapter clearly speaks of the purpose of God's predestination, saying that it is "unto sonship" (v. 5).

The Brethren also taught about sonship, but the sonship they taught is not by birth but by adoption. What they meant is that we are not genuine sons of God but adopted sons of God; hence, we have obtained sonship through God's adoption. However, we must see that the phrase *predestinating us unto sonship* is included in the outline above as: "To work Himself, in His Divine Trinity, into His chosen ones." How can God cause us to have sonship? He has to work Himself into us. How does He carry this out? It is through His Divine Trinity. Hence, Ephesians chapter one begins by telling us how God works Himself into us through His Divine Trinity that we may obtain sonship (vv. 3-14).

If we carefully study Romans 8 and Galatians 4 again, we will see that God's enabling us to receive sonship is not a simple matter. First, God the Father had to send His beloved Son to accomplish redemption for us that we may be qualified to receive sonship (Rom. 8:3; Gal. 4:4-5). Next, God the Father also sent the Spirit of sonship into our heart that we may cry, "Abba, Father!" (v. 6), and that in this Spirit we may live out the reality of the sonship. Sonship in Ephesians 1:5 implies the Triune God's working Himself into us. How can we be qualified to be sons of God unless the Triune God works Himself into us? Do not think that God has merely adopted some of us, who were captives of sins, to be His sons by capturing us out of Satan's hand and cleansing us with His precious blood. No, God has *begotten* us (John 1:13; 1 John 5:1) that we may be His children; this implies that the Triune God has wrought Himself into us.

We know it is very spontaneous for us who are children to call our own parents "father" and "mother" because we are born of them, but it is not so spontaneous to call our parents-in-law "father" and "mother" because we do not have a life relationship with them. When our parents *begot* us, they wrought themselves into us; that is, they passed on their life and nature to us. We are Chinese not by adoption but by birth because our ancestors were Chinese. Likewise, we must have the assurance that we are the real sons of God in life because we are born of Him with His life; thus, we have a life relationship with Him. Since we are not adopted sons, it is normal and sweet when we call God, "Father." We must realize that the central move of God in His economy revealed in the Bible is that God wants to work Himself into us, His chosen ones, through His Divine Trinity.

In order to work Himself into His chosen ones, God must be the Spirit. Moreover, the ultimate consummation and manifestation of the Triune God must also be the Spirit. The Divine Trinity has been processed. God the Father is the source of the Divine Trinity (John 13:3; 1 Cor. 6:19). God the Son is the embodiment of the processed Triune God (Col. 2:9); He passed through the processes of incarnation, human living, crucifixion, resurrection, and ascension and eventually became the all-inclusive, life-giving Spirit (1 Cor. 15:45b) as the ultimate consummation of the processed Triune God. All that the Divine Trinity has is consummated in the Spirit—the processed, compounded, all-inclusive, life-giving, indwelling, sevenfold intensified, and ultimately consummated Spirit.

The Bible says that God is Spirit (John 4:24); moreover, the ultimate manifestation of the Father, the Son, and the Spirit is the Spirit (Matt. 28:19). God can come into us because He is Spirit. On the other hand, He had to create us with a spirit. God is not only Spirit in His Divine Trinity but also ultimately became the Spirit. He created us also with a spirit so that He as God who is Spirit may come into us human beings with a spirit, so that the two spirits—our spirit and His Spirit—may be joined as one spirit.

There are three places in the New Testament that mention both the Spirit of God and our human spirit. The first place is John 3:6: "That which is born of the Spirit is spirit." This shows the Spirit begetting the spirit. The second place is John 4:24: "God is Spirit, and those who worship Him must worship in spirit and truthfulness." This speaks about the spirit worshipping the Spirit. The third place is Romans 8:16: "The Spirit Himself witnesses with our spirit that we are children of God." This is the Spirit with the spirit. The Spirit begets the spirit, the spirit worships the Spirit, and the Spirit witnesses with the spirit. We have a human spirit within us. When our human spirit is regenerated by the Holy Spirit, we can worship God as Spirit with our regenerated spirit. Moreover, the two spirits witness as one spirit.

This is the way God works Himself into us. In His Divine Trinity, in His ultimate consummation, God reaches us and comes into us as the Spirit. Not only the Spirit comes, but the

Son and the Father also come. Furthermore, when He comes, He does not come into our body of blood and flesh, into our internal organs, such as the stomach. Neither does He come into our mind, emotion, or will. Instead, He comes into our spirit, which is the innermost part, the center, the most sincere part of our being, to be joined with us. Eventually, these two spirits are joined and mingled as one. Hence, 1 Corinthians 6:17 says, "But he who is joined to the Lord is one spirit." This is the primary matter in God's economy. At this point, God has wrought Himself into His chosen ones in His Divine Trinity.

C. That They May Become His Children as His Sons with His Life and Nature to Become His House So That He May Have a Dwelling Place for His Rest

When God works Himself into us, He makes us His children as His sons. According to the Greek, in the New Testament there is only one place—2 Corinthians 6:18—that says we are God's sons and daughters. There are many places, however, that say we are God's children (John 1:12; Acts 13:33; Rom. 8:16; Gal. 4:28; Phil. 2:15; 1 John 3:1-2, 10). Logically, only sons are sons; daughters are not sons. Strictly speaking, God has sons only; He does not have daughters. We are all His children. As such, we must exercise to be led by His Spirit continually that we may grow in life and arrive at the stage of being His sons (Rom. 8:14). Sisters, when you live and act in spirit, you are sons of God. Ultimately, when we are fully matured, we become God's legal heirs to receive our inheritance (v. 17).

By being born of God we have our Father God's life and nature (John 17:2; 2 Pet. 1:4) to become His house. Both in Greek and in Chinese, the word *house* has two denotations. On the one hand, it denotes the family, the household (Eph. 2:19); on the other hand, it denotes a habitation, a dwelling place (v. 22). On the one hand, we are God's household as members of God's house, God's family; on the other hand, we are God's dwelling place on earth, and we have God dwelling in our spirit. God obtains a dwelling place for His rest within us.

We must realize that if there were not a group of people who allowed God to work Himself into them, God would become homeless. In the Old Testament time, God sighed through the prophet, saying, "Heaven is My throne, / And the earth the footstool for My feet. / Where then is the house that you will build for Me, / And where is the place of My rest?" (Isa. 66:1). Neither heaven nor earth is God's house. It is true that some passages in the Bible say that God's dwelling place is in heaven (1 Kings 8:39; 2 Chron. 6:21; Isa. 26:21; 63:15), but heaven is only His temporary dwelling place, His temporary tabernacle. Why does God still dwell in His heavenly tabernacle? It is because the building of His dwelling place has not yet been completed. Therefore, both in the Old Testament and in the New Testament, God voices His longing for a dwelling place. At the most He only has a throne and footstool; He does not have a home. He is longing to have a home as His dwelling place. As one who knew God's desire, David wrote a psalm to God, saying, "I shall not go into the tent of my house; / I shall not go up onto the couch of my bed; / I shall not give sleep to my eyes, / Slumber to my eyelids; / Until I find a place for Jehovah, / A tabernacle for the Mighty One of Jacob" (Psa. 132:3-5). David desired to find a resting place for God; only then could he have peace deep within. It is the same in the New Testament—God's house has yet to be completed. Therefore, in John 14 the Lord Jesus said that He had to go to build an abode (vv. 2, 23). This means that through His death and resurrection (that is, His going and coming) He would bring man into God that man may be prepared to become God's dwelling place. This dwelling place is the church, the unique habitation of God, the living habitation built by God with His redeemed people.

D. That They May Have an Organic Union with the Divine Trinity in Christ to Become the Members of Christ That Constitute His Body as the Corporate Expression of the Triune God in Christ

God works Himself into us that we may have an organic union with the Divine Trinity in Christ to become the members

of Christ that constitute His Body as the corporate expression
of the Triune God in Christ. We need at least thirty Scripture
passages to explain this matter. I intentionally omitted the
Bible references pertaining to "in Christ," "Divine Trinity,"
and "organic union" because I want you to study and find
them. In our organic union with the Divine Trinity we become
the members of Christ; that is, we become His bone and His
flesh (Eph. 5:30-32). Collectively, as members of Christ we
are constituted into one Body as a corporate expression of the
Triune God in Christ.

We, the regenerated believers, can become God's house and
God's dwelling place because firstly we have been chosen by
God in Christ (1:4). That we are in Christ refers not only to a
change in our position in our being transferred by God out of
Adam into Christ (1 Cor. 1:30; 4:15; 2 Cor. 5:17; Rom. 8:1). It
also refers to the daily subjective and continual experience in
our regenerated spirit; that is, through our organic union
with the Divine Trinity we share His life and His nature and
have one living and one move with Him.

The believers are joined to God the Father by repenting
unto Him (Acts 2:38; 26:18), by being baptized into Him (Matt.
28:19b), and by being born of Him to become His children
(John 1:12-13; James 1:18; 1 John 3:1). The believers are joined
to God the Son by being identified with Him in His death
(Rom. 6:3b, 6a; Gal. 2:20a; Col. 2:20a), in His burial (Rom.
6:4a; Col. 2:12a), in His being made alive (Eph. 2:5; Col.
2:13b), in His resurrection (Eph. 2:6a; Rom. 6:4b; Col. 2:12b;
3:1a), and in His ascension (Eph. 2:6b). On the one hand, the
believers are joined to God the Spirit by receiving Him essentially as the Holy Spirit (John 20:22), the Spirit of life (Rom.
8:2), the life-giving Spirit (1 Cor. 15:45), for their existence,
their being, their life, and their living; on the other hand, they
are joined to God the Spirit by being baptized into Him economically to receive Him as the Spirit of power (Acts 1:8a;
Luke 24:49b) for their spiritual work and function that they
may witness for the Lord and spread forth His gospel. Hence,
the believers need to be joined to God the Spirit essentially
as the Spirit of life and also economically as the Spirit of

power. The union we have with the Divine Trinity in different aspects is as organic as the grafting of a branch to the tree.

We are a wild olive tree (Rom. 11:17-24), and the Divine Trinity is the cultivated olive tree. Originally, the two—He and we—are two different trees, each having its own life. But now these two trees are grafted together so that two lives have become one life. This enables us to continually enjoy the riches of the Divine Trinity. As a result, we become the members of Christ (1 Cor. 12:12; Eph. 5:30), the branches of the true vine (John 15:1, 5) to constitute His Body, which is the church. Ephesians 1:22b-23 says, "The church, which is His Body, the fullness of the One who fills all in all." The church as the Body of Christ is an organism constituted with all those who have been regenerated by God with the divine life to be the fullness of Christ for His expression. Since Christ is the embodiment of the Triune God, when He is expressed, the Triune God is also expressed. Eventually, the church becomes the corporate expression of the Triune God in Christ. This is the economy of God.

A WORD OF BURDEN

Brothers and sisters, you all must clearly see the economy of God. In the outline I did not mention anything about sin, sinners, the devil, or Satan. Today if you ask Christians, "What is the economy of God?", some Christians who have studied theology will say, "There are two great needs of man today. First, as sinners, we need God's salvation; second, we have been ensnared and troubled by the devil, so we need God to destroy the works of the devil. Therefore, the first step of God's plan is to save sinners, because 1 Timothy 1:15 says, 'Faithful is the word and worthy of all acceptance, that Christ Jesus came into the world to save sinners.' The next step is to destroy the works of Satan, because 1 John 3:8 says, 'For this purpose the Son of God was manifested, that He might destroy the works of the devil.'" This is what most Christians know concerning the economy of God.

When I was young, I thought about human life and considered it to be a real suffering. But I did not, nor did I dare to, blame God. I only blamed myself that I was born a sinner.

Who taught me to lie? I knew how to lie by birth. My mother always taught me to tell the truth, yet the more she taught me, the more I lied. Who taught me to hate? I knew how to hate by birth. My mother taught me to love my brothers and sisters, but the more she taught me, the more I had jealousy and hatred instead of love. Because the financial situation of our family was not so good, sometimes our relatives or friends would give us some gifts. When my mother was distributing candies to us, I wished I could get at least half of them; I was unhappy when I received less. Who taught me this? I knew it by birth. Therefore, it is troublesome to be a sinner, and it is truly not easy to be freed from the entanglement of sin. Not only so, the devil also follows us. We are not able to do good things, but we are fully able to do bad things without being taught. Whose work is this? How is it done? We all have a heart to go upward, and we resolve in our hearts to excel by strenuous efforts, yet our feet are always going downward. Who is doing this in us? It is the combined work of two parties, the sinner and the devil.

You cannot deny that the sinner is you, but you can also say that the sinner is not you. This is really difficult to discern. Ancient Chinese scholars debated whether human nature is good or bad. Mencius advocated that man is naturally good, whereas Hsun-tzu advocated that man is naturally evil. Actually, we are both good and evil. Speaking of our good nature, we human beings are truly good; we like to honor and obey our parents. In the morning we may love them, yet in the evening we may provoke them to anger. Therefore, it is difficult to say whether man is good or evil. This is the result of the trouble brought in by sin and the devil.

Christianity pays much attention to these two things. They preach that Hebrews 2:14 tells us since we have shared in blood and flesh, He also Himself in like manner partook of the same, that through death He might destroy him who has the might of death, that is, the devil. They consider that this is the economy of God. However, this is not the economy of God; this is only the procedure to reach the goal of God's economy. In order to accomplish His economy, God has to deal with the sinner and destroy the works of the devil. The economy of God is that He wants to work Himself as the Triune God into us that we may become His house so that He may have a home, a dwelling place for His rest, and that we may become the Body of Christ for His own expression. This is what Christianity has not seen. This is my burden; I have not spoken enough about this matter. Although I have published many books about this, I still have many messages within me ready to be released.

Most people in Christianity not only do not see the economy of God, but they do not even see clearly the truth about the sinner and the devil. Some even oppose me for saying that there is sin within man (Rom. 7:17, 20), because they believe that within man there is no sin. This is really pitiful. A peach tree is a peach tree because it has the element of the peach. Likewise, man is a sinner because he has sin within him. How can man be a sinner if he does not have sin in him? I went further to say that the sin within man is the sinful nature of Satan (cf. John 8:44). In Romans 7, Paul personified sin, saying that it is revived (v. 9) and very active and that it can deceive and kill people (v. 11). Therefore, sin is not only living, but it is also a person. Who is this person? Sin cannot be Adam; it is the evil nature of Satan, the evil one. When I said this, it caused more to oppose me. They said that the reason I said Satan is in man is that I am demon-possessed. When I heard that, I was annoyed and amused at the same time. They said this because they have been deceived by Satan and therefore do not recognize that Satan is in them.

This does not mean that today we should not speak about sinners or forgiveness of sins, but our goal is the economy of God. To illustrate, before we can meet in the meeting hall, first we must sweep the floor, clean the yard, wipe the table, and arrange the chairs in an orderly fashion. However, our purpose is not cleaning but meeting. The economy of God is very lofty. How lofty is it? It is lofty to such an extent that we are being made God. Some will say, "You are speaking heresy again; you are teaching polytheism. How can we become God?" But this is a fact. God's desire is to work in us to the extent that we are as honorable and glorious as He is; we have His life and nature but we have no share in His

Godhead. Now He is doing a transforming and conforming work within us; in the future He will come again to glorify our body. The Bible says clearly that we do not know what we will be, but one thing we know is that at His coming back we will be like Him because He will make us exactly like Him (1 John 3:2). Of course, we do not participate in His Godhead to become the object of worship; this is the difference between us and Him. I hope that you all can have a proper understanding concerning this matter.

CHAPTER SIX

THE REALIZATION AND EXPERIENCE
OF GOD'S ECONOMY

Scripture Reading: Matt. 1:23, 21, 18; John 12:24; Rom. 8:29;
2 Cor. 13:14; Eph. 1:4, 7, 13; 3:17-19; Rev. 1:4-5; Matt. 16:16, 18

We have fellowshipped about two major points relating to the revelation and the vision of God: concerning the Divine Trinity and the economy of God. In the previous chapter we saw four points concerning the economy of God. In this chapter I will speak particularly about our need for the subjective realization and experience of the Divine Trinity and of the church. After seeing the preceding four points, we will sense a need—that we should not only study the so-called truths and visions, but we should also pay attention to the realization, knowledge, and experience of these matters. In other words, we should not just see the facts recorded in the Bible, but we should also realize and experience them.

THE REALIZATION, KNOWLEDGE, AND EXPERIENCE
OF GOD'S ECONOMY

If we really see the vision, we will certainly respond with an inner desire to realize, know, and experience God's economy. We can see from the very beginning of the New Testament, in Matthew chapter one, that the Triune God desires to dispense Himself into man.

A. The Lord Jesus as the Prototype
of the Mingling of God and Man

In Matthew 1, we can see at least four facts: the genealogy of Jesus, the conception of Jesus, the birth of Jesus, and the name of Jesus. However, the most important thing concerning

Matthew 1 is not just to see these facts but to see a precious vision in these facts and to make that vision our experience. We must realize and experience these facts. Take for example these three words: *the Lord Jesus.* If you read them one by one separately, it is difficult to understand what they mean. But if you put them together and read them, then you can discover their meaning. By the same principle, in Matthew 1 several facts are presented here to speak forth a reality, and this reality is that the Triune God wants to work Himself into man.

1. The Vision in Matthew 1

First, we must see that Matthew 1 mentions God (v. 23); it mentions the Son (v. 21), Jesus, who was God incarnated and born to be a man; it also mentions the Spirit (v. 18) as the basic essence and element of the virgin Mary's pregnancy. Moreover, this chapter refers to Jehovah because *Je* in *Jesus* is a shortened form of *Jehovah,* and *sus* means Savior or salvation; furthermore, Jesus is the One who is called the Christ (v. 18). Thus, this one chapter mentions God, the Son, the Spirit, Jehovah, the Savior or salvation, and Christ. Anyone who studies the Bible can see these divine titles. But we still need to see a vision here.

2. The Purpose of God's Creation of Man Being for Man to Have His Life

Originally, God was outside of man. He created man in His image and according to His likeness, and then He breathed into man the breath of life, giving man life and breath. God did not do these two things when He created the animals, or even when He created the angels. He created man in His own image and breathed His own breath, the breath of life, into man. It was truly special that He did this. However, God was still outside of man; He was He, and man was man. Despite this, these two were of the same kind. In Genesis 1 when God created all the living things, everything was "according to their kind." Today those who graft trees know that trees of different species cannot be grafted together; only trees of the same species can be grafted. In His creation, God did a work of preparation beforehand; that is, He created man to be of His kind with the view of having man enter into a relationship with Him just like the relationship of grafting.

Later in the Bible the Lord Jesus Himself definitely told us that He is the true vine and we are the branches (John 15:1, 5). But we must realize that we were not born as branches of the vine. Rather, we were wild branches (Rom. 11:17, 24), and it is by faith that we have been grafted into Him as the vine (v. 20, cf. v. 23). This means that although we and the Lord Jesus are different "trees," we are of the same species. At the very least, we have the same image as God and bear His likeness. But despite the fact that we are of the same species with God, He is still He, and we are still we. He is outside of us, and we are outside of Him. In life and nature, and especially in essence, we and He are completely unrelated.

Please forgive me for saying that this point is the greatest deficiency in Christianity's theology. There is a school in Christianity called Reformed Theology. Those who belong to this school absolutely deny that we saved ones have the divine nature inwardly; they mainly acknowledge that we have been reformed. They say that originally we were very evil, but now we have been reformed; similarly, society was once evil, but now it has been reformed and improved. In the last century, this kind of teaching was very prevailing. This group of people advocated that this world, instead of getting worse and worse, would become better and better. Therefore, the world would become a utopia even before the return of the Lord Jesus. A utopia is an ideal kingdom in which everyone is happy and everything is good. Despite the fact that there is evil today, the day will come in which nothing is evil and everything becomes a utopia. How can this happen? First, it is by preaching the gospel to lead people to reform their errors and revert to good deeds through repentance; second, it is by teaching the biblical truths to exhort the believers to reform themselves. But since the biblical truths have not yet spread to the entire world, everyone must do their best to preach the gospel and bring people to repentance. However, this group of people pays no attention to regeneration; they only emphasize teaching the truth to change human society and turn it into a utopia, an ideal world.

At the end of the last century, this school of theology was very prevailing and strongly influential in Europe. But at the beginning of this century, in 1914, war broke out in Europe, and the fighting was very severe. This struck a heavy blow against the Reformed Theology. After the war in Europe, European theology put particular emphasis on the study of prophecies. At that time, the Lord's recovery was just being raised up in China. Many of the spiritual books I read came from Europe, and they were all concerning prophecies. That was because people all felt that the world was becoming more and more chaotic and more and more evil, so they would no longer listen to teachings about utopia. Instead, they had to see what the Bible said. Later the world situation became even worse. In 1931 Japan invaded the northeastern part of China, and war broke out again. Then Italy invaded Ethiopia, and Hitler invaded the countries bordering Germany. By 1939 Europe was embroiled in another great war that eventually developed into the Second World War, which covered an even greater area and was more severe than the First World War. After this, nobody believed in the Reformed Theology anymore.

Today, however, forty years after the last great war, this school seems to be showing signs of gradually raising its head again. It still emphasizes that Christians have only one nature and do not have another nature inwardly. Also, it emphasizes that regeneration is merely to change a person's original nature. This is just like what the Chinese mean when they say that we have to "daily turn over a new leaf" and "develop our bright virtue" so that we would become "renewed people"; this means that we have reformed ourselves. Having been influenced by such a doctrine and having accepted it, many seminary students in America do not believe that Christians have two natures and two lives. The Bible, however, clearly states that when we are regenerated, we are born of the Spirit (John 3:6) and we have received the life and nature of God into us (vv. 15-16, 36; 2 Pet. 1:4) to make us a new creation. This is not merely reforming man's original nature.

The reason I am speaking so much about this matter is that I want to show you that many Christians today are not at all clear about what regeneration is. Twenty years ago when I first went to America, I released a message telling people that we need regeneration not just because we are fallen, but that even if Adam had not fallen, even if all men had not fallen and had not the slightest bit of sin, we would still need to be regenerated. Take the example of grafting. Grafting is not done because a tree has fallen and therefore one of its branches has to be cut off and grafted into a tree that has not fallen. We all know that grafting has nothing to do with whether or not a tree is fallen. Grafting is a matter of the inward life and nature. Even though you as a tree and the Lord Jesus as a tree are of the same species, your life and nature are too poor, so you need to be grafted into the Lord Jesus, whose life and nature are the best. This is why in Genesis 2 before man had fallen, God placed him in front of the tree of life. God meant to tell man that he had a life within which was merely the human life and not the divine life. Therefore, God put man in front of the tree of life that man might receive the life of the tree of life, which is a higher life.

In Matthew 1:21, the angel of the Lord told Joseph in a dream, "She [Mary] will bear a son, and you shall call His name Jesus, for it is He who will save His people from their sins." It is true that the problem of sin is here. But we must realize that our need for the life of God is recorded in Genesis 2 before sin had come in; sin did not come in until Genesis 3. This proves that it is not because of our fall that we need God to come into us; instead, it is something originally ordained by God. God created us as His vessels (Rom. 9:20-24) to contain Him. Romans 9 says that we are vessels of mercy, then we will become vessels unto honor, and eventually we will be vessels unto glory. The honor of a vessel does not depend upon the vessel itself but upon its content. When man was created, God did not immediately get into him; hence, at the most man was a vessel of mercy in which there was no God, much less glory. Today, however, we have God, so we have become vessels unto honor; in the future when we are in glory, we will become vessels unto glory.

The purpose of a vessel is to contain things. A vessel may have fallen into the garbage can due to carelessness, but that does not mean that it is no longer a vessel and does not need to contain things. It is true that because we had fallen into the garbage can of sin and had become dirty, we needed God to wash us clean. But God's purpose in cleansing us is that we may contain Him. In this respect, even if we had not fallen into the garbage can of sin and we had been clean, yet without God being put inside of us, we would still be empty. We need to be filled with God. This is the purpose of God's creation of man revealed in the Bible.

3. The Lord Jesus Being the Mingling of God with Man

Therefore, Matthew 1 does not simply tell us how God was conceived within the virgin Mary through the Holy Spirit and born as the Son, Jesus, who is Jehovah the Savior and whose name is called Emmanuel (which is translated, God with us). Everyone understands this doctrine, but very few people have seen the vision portrayed by this doctrine. This vision is that the Triune God worked Himself into man and was mingled with man. This God is Triune (Gen. 1:26); He is the Father, the Angel of Jehovah (Christ—Exo. 3:2-15), and the Spirit of God (Gen. 1:2). In the Old Testament, however, this Triune God had not yet entered into man. At the most He descended upon the judges and prophets as the Spirit of Jehovah (Judg. 3:10; 6:34; Ezek. 11:5). It was at the beginning of the New Testament that we are clearly told that the Triune God entered into man and was mingled with man.

The Lord Jesus became flesh to be a genuine man. The basic element of His becoming a man was the mingling of the divine essence (the Holy Spirit) with the human essence. According to the record in the Gospel of Matthew, the Holy Spirit as the divine essence entered into Mary and was mingled with her human essence to give birth to a God-man. The One who was brought forth from her was not only a man but also God. Isaiah 9:6 says, "For a child is born to us... / His name will be called... / Mighty God." The baby born in the manger was the Mighty God. Therefore, the Lord Jesus was not only a man but also God; He had both divinity and humanity. He was the mingling of divinity with humanity.

The Lord Jesus is the mingling of two natures—the divine nature and the human nature—without a third nature being produced; on the contrary, the two natures continue to exist distinctly. This is typified by the mingling of oil with fine flour (Lev. 2:4). When oil and fine flour are mingled together, the element of the oil and the element of the fine flour both continue to exist individually, without a third nature being produced as the result of a chemical reaction. This is not like the chemical process in which a neutral substance is produced when a base is added to an acid. Furthermore, mingling is different from union. Union is where two are merely joined together; mingling is where one enters into another, and the two are mingled together. The Holy Spirit entered into Mary's womb and was mingled with humanity to give birth to One who was the expression of two in one, the expression of God and man, and whose name was called Jesus. Thus, the Lord Jesus was born a God-man as the mingling of God with man. In Him were both divinity and humanity. He was the complete God and the perfect man. This is a divine and mysterious matter in the Bible.

B. The Church Being the Aggregate of the Mingling of God with Man

Today many Christians know that the church should exist, and their creeds also speak of the Triune God and the church, but they have not seen that the church is a product of the Triune God's entering into man and being mingled with man. The Triune God and the church are two great visions that we should see. The church is an aggregate entity produced out of God's working Himself into man in His Divine Trinity.

God entered into man and produced this model, which was first seen in Matthew 1 as an individual, the Lord Jesus. Later this individual model passed through death and entered into resurrection; when this model came out in resurrection, He was not just an individual. This is what the Lord Himself said: "Unless the grain of wheat falls into the ground and dies, it abides alone; but if it dies, it bears much fruit"

(John 12:24). By this time, this model became a corporate product which is the church (Heb. 2:12; John 20:17, 19-23). In Matthew 1 an individual mingling of God and man was produced, but when this One was resurrected, all the ones chosen by God were included in Him and resurrected together with Him (Eph. 2:6; 1 Pet. 1:3) to become the corporate mingling of God with man. Regardless of whether it is the individual model or the corporate product, the principle is the same: the Triune God enters into man and mingles with man.

Christianity today has not seen this matter. I do not only preach this truth, but I have also written books about it. Up until today, only slanderous people say that I am teaching heresy. Not one person with a degree and proper qualifications has written anything refuting this truth. In the Los Angeles area, there is a group of opposers who organized a research group to study the verses we quoted in order to refute our teachings. After studying Isaiah 9, they had to admit that Jesus truly is the Father.

C. The Center of the Entire Bible— the Triune God Working Himself into Man and Mingling with Man to Produce the Church

1. In God's Creation in the Old Testament

I have spoken so much because I have a burden to show you that our God is the Triune God and His heart's desire, His longing, in eternity has been to work Himself into man. The Bible with its sixty-six books is very rich in content, but its emphasis is very simple: the Triune God wants to work Himself into man. The first step He took to accomplish this purpose was to create man in His image and according to His likeness as a preparation for Him to work Himself into man. We all know that when a vessel is created to contain something, the vessel must be made the same as the thing it will contain. If the thing is square, you cannot make a triangular vessel. If the thing is triangular, you cannot make a round vessel. From the beginning, God planned to put Himself into man. Therefore, in the beginning when He created man, He created man the same as He. This was God's preparation.

2. *In Incarnation*

After approximately four thousand years, God finally came to enter into the man whom He had created. The way He came was not by force; He did not come by using His sovereignty or His great power. He came according to the principle of life in His creation. He first entered into man and was conceived in the womb of the virgin Mary, and then He remained there for nine months before being born on the earth. God is the almighty God who gives life to the dead and calls the things not being as being (Rom. 4:17); why did He not get into man immediately, be born immediately, and grow up to be the God-man Jesus immediately? He did not do it this way. He entered into man by keeping the principle He had established when He created all things. Thus, He was in Mary's womb for nine months before being born as a child. After His birth, He grew up day by day also according to the principle of life. The Bible records this very clearly: "And Jesus advanced in wisdom and stature and in the grace manifested in Him before God and men" (Luke 2:52). Then, again, when He was thirty years old, He came out to minister according to God's ordained principle (Num. 4:3; 1 Chron. 23:3; Luke 3:23) and did the work which God had commissioned Him to do. This shows that every step of the living of the Lord Jesus on earth was according to the principle of life. He lived on earth neither by miracles nor by His sovereign authority but completely according to the natural laws of the growth of human life. This was the second step of God's working Himself into man.

3. *In the Lord Jesus' Death and Resurrection*

After thirty-three and a half years, again, according to God's ordination, the Lord Jesus entered into death and then rose from the dead. When He entered into death, Satan thought it was he who had captured the Lord Jesus, put Him on the cross, and crucified Him there. However, in God's eyes, it was the Lord who willingly laid down His own life to accomplish redemption (John 10:18). He put Himself into death and resurrected from the dead. This was the third step He took to work Himself into man. Through death and resurrection, the Triune God is able to dispense Himself into the myriads of people that He has chosen. This, however, is from God's point of view. From man's point of view, the saved ones, the believers, still need to go to preach and announce the Lord who died and resurrected so that, one by one, all those chosen by God throughout the ages may believe into Him.

In God's eyes, on the day that the Lord Jesus resurrected, we all were also resurrected in Him (Eph. 2:6). But in our experience, we believe in the Lord and are saved one by one in time. Today, by the Lord's mercy, although our practice of door-knocking according to the God-ordained way is very effective, it is also very tiring. We should expend all our strength because this is according to the law of God's ordination. In principle, all those chosen by God will come. If we had not been chosen by God, no matter how much people preached to us, we would not have believed. But once we believe into Him, He comes into us and we enter into Him. Then we are baptized into Him and have an organic union with Him (Gal. 3:27; Rom. 6:3; Matt. 28:19; 1 Cor. 12:13; 6:17). Thus, the Triune God is mingled with us.

4. In Paul's Epistles

The divine revelation concerning the Triune God desiring to work Himself into man extends throughout the entire New Testament. From Matthew to Revelation, every book was written according to this principle. The four Gospels were written according to the principle of the Triune God's working Himself into man. Acts also shows us this principle, and none of the Epistles is an exception to this rule. Let us take Romans as an example. Romans 1 speaks of the gospel of God, which is a gospel of the forgiveness of sins, a gospel of justification by faith. Then Romans 8 speaks about God coming into us. Verses 9 and 10 say that the Spirit of God dwells in us, that we have the Spirit of Christ in us as the indwelling Spirit, and that Christ is in us. Here we see God, Christ the Son, and the Spirit; we see the Triune God. This is different from the Old Testament. In the Old Testament the Triune God was outside of man; by Romans 8, the three of the Triune God are all in man. This is also different from Matthew 1. When Matthew 1 speaks of God's entering into man, it is individual; by Romans 8, God's entering into man is corporate. This can be proven by Romans 8:29 where it says that Christ is the Firstborn among many brothers. The many brothers are we who have God in us.

If we continue reading, we come to 1 and 2 Corinthians. At the conclusion of 2 Corinthians Paul blesses the believers with the blessed Triune God: "The grace of the Lord Jesus Christ and the love of God and the fellowship of the Holy Spirit be with you all" (13:14). The Triune God is with us and in us.

Then in Ephesians, the first chapter begins with God the Father's selection and predestination (vv. 3-6), God the Son's redemption (vv. 7-12), and God the Spirit's sealing and pledging (vv. 13-14). The result is that, by His transmission to the church, the Triune God enters into us to produce the Body, which is the fullness of the One who fills all in all (vv. 22-23). This is God's economy. This means that God's economy is to dispense the Triune God into man to produce a result, which is the church as His Body, the fullness of the One who fills all in all. In Ephesians 3 Paul says that he bowed his knees unto the Father and asked that He would grant us to be strengthened with power through His Spirit into the inner man that Christ may make His home in our hearts through faith (vv. 14-17). The result is that we are filled unto all the fullness of God (vv. 18-19). This is the dispensing of the Triune God into our entire being, resulting in our becoming the fullness, the expression, of God. What is spoken of in all the Epistles ultimately is related to this matter.

5. In John's Revelation

Finally, in Revelation, at the very beginning it says, "Grace to you and peace from Him who is and who was and who is coming, and from the seven Spirits who are before His throne, and from Jesus Christ" (1:4-5). This indicates that the processed Triune God, including all that the eternal Father is, all that the sevenfold intensified Spirit does, and all that the anointed Son has obtained and attained, has been dispensed into the believers with the result that the golden lampstands are produced to be His corporate testimony (vv. 9, 11, 20). At the end of Revelation, in chapter twenty-two, again we see "a river of water of life, bright as crystal, proceeding out of the throne of God and of the Lamb in the middle of its street" (v. 1). Here we have God, the Lamb (the Son), and the Spirit (signified by the river of water of life). This depicts how the Triune God dispenses Himself into His redeemed under His headship. Then in verse 17, the Spirit and the bride say, "Come!" This means that the Spirit and the bride, having become one, speak as one. The Spirit is the ultimate consummation of the Triune God, who has worked Himself into us and constituted us into a corporate bride. In other words, the Triune God is the Husband, and we who have been filled and transformed by Him become His bride to be one with Him. This is the most important matter, and the central matter as well, revealed to us in the entire Bible.

D. Experiencing the Dispensing of the Triune God in Our Practical Living to Manifest the Reality of the Church

I repeat, my burden is not merely to show you the crucial points; it is not enough just to do that. You must have the realization and the experience. But how do we have the realization and the experience? It is not at all difficult. Many Christians feel it is hard because they have been influenced by wrong teachings. When the teaching is wrong, it is very difficult to have the realization and experience. If we have the proper knowledge of the truth that the Triune God is in us and is united and mingled with us, then it is very easy to experience this truth.

1. Praying with Our Spirit to Contact the Triune God

When a saved person feels he has the Lord's presence inwardly, that means the Spirit is in him. Where the Spirit is, there the Lord is (1 Cor. 6:17; 2 Cor. 3:17), and where the Lord is, there the Father is (Rom. 8:9-10). The three are all in the believers; when One comes, all three of Them come. This is because the Spirit is the reality, the realization, of the Son (John 14:17), and the Son is the embodiment of the Father (10:30; 14:10-11). Thus, the three are really just the One, but this One has the aspect of being three distinctly.

I am from Shantung Province, so I have eaten wheat for eighty years. If today you ask me what the element in wheat really is, I still do not know. If I must understand wheat to eat it, then I would have died long ago. Recently, I started to like eating yogurt. My wife probably understands what its ingredients are, because she pays close attention to nutrition, but I do not know anything about it. I only know how to eat and enjoy it. Some days I wake up at 4:30 in the morning, and I begin working in my head while I am in bed. When 6:00 comes, I get up and continue working. By 7:20 I am hungry. Then I eat some yogurt which is nutritious and easy to digest and assimilate. As soon as I have eaten it, my entire being is refreshed and satisfied. Today we have the best "yogurt" within us, which is the Triune God. What is He like? It is hard for us to describe. The Father is the Son, and the Son is the embodiment of the Father; the Son is realized in the Spirit, and the Spirit is the reality of the Son. What is this all about? I have spoken about it for decades, and I can only speak according to the Bible. I still do not know fully what the mystery of the Triune God is all about.

My point is this: While you are here being trained, you should not just be learning the truth; it is even more important for you to learn to eat the "yogurt" every day, to enjoy the Triune God daily. To eat the physical yogurt, you do not use your nose or your ears; rather, you use your mouth. Likewise, to enjoy the Triune God, you do not need to work your brain, use your ears, or bow down before the Lord. You just need to use your spirit, open your heart, and open your mouth to pray to the Lord; then you will be able to enjoy Him.

2. Exercising Our Spirit
to Call on the Name of the Lord
to Enjoy the Triune God

You are being trained here to learn how to use your spirit.

From the time you get up in the morning, you must learn to use your spirit. This is just like when you want to breathe, there is no need for you to beg others or expect any kind of help. You just need to exercise your breathing organs; once you inhale through your nose, the air gets right in. In the same principle, if you want to enjoy the Triune God, you need to exercise your spirit. For example, as soon as you get up in the morning, you feel that you are tired. The more you think about it, the more tired you feel. But if you immediately turn from that condition back to your spirit, then your entire being will be revived. The secret of turning to your spirit is to call, "O Lord Jesus! O Lord Jesus!" You do not need to call loudly. When you call softly from the depths of your being, immediately you will return to your spirit, and your entire being will be revived.

3. Experiencing God's Salvation and Dealing with the Enemy by Turning to Our Spirit

I believe that when you are living together with others, you will face many troubles as soon as you get up in the morning. This is because Satan has many messengers. Many times the sisters who are your roommates can give you many problems. For example, you have just gotten up, and your roommate at that exact moment breaks your toothbrush mug. You dare not lose your temper, but you are very angry inwardly. At this time, you just need to call, "O Lord Jesus! O Lord Jesus!" The more you call, the less you will be bothered. Instead, you will feel that inwardly you have the enjoyment and the watering. I believe that to some extent you all have had this kind of experience. You must know that Satan always stirs up some trouble in our environment to disturb us and force us into anger. When you are angry, Satan is happy. Moreover, when you are angry, all the truths that you have ever heard become nothing; they are all made void and vanish into thin air. Everything you have heard about the Triune God and God's salvation are all gone. You are here being trained and have heard so many truths and received so many visions, but because of Satan's bothering, whatever you have learned all leaks out.

Matthew 1:21 says, "Jesus...will save His people from their sins." Christianity explains this verse by saying that the Lord Jesus washed away our sins through His crucifixion and the shedding of His precious blood. I dare not say that this is not so, but this is only dealing with our sinful deeds. On the positive side, the Lord still wants to save us from the power of sin. We must know that the Lord Jesus has two names: *Jesus* is Jehovah, and *Emmanuel* is God. This indicates that the Lord Jesus is both Jehovah and God. He saves us from our sins mainly by becoming the Spirit to enter into us to save us from the power of sin.

According to the preceding example, when a sister breaks your toothbrush mug and you get angry, is that sin? And if another sister tracks dirt all over the floor which you had scrubbed clean the previous night, will you get angry? Then another sister carelessly gets her hands, which are greasy with vegetable oil, all over your hair, which you just washed the night before, what will you do? Do you experience Jesus saving you from your sins? I believe that if each time you would call, "O Lord Jesus! O Lord Jesus," instead of getting angry, you will be full of the enjoyment of the Lord. This is your realization, your experience. The result of such realization and experience is that you have the real enjoyment of the Triune God. Consequently, the church is produced. However, if Satan comes to disturb you and you are defeated, and if he comes again, and you are defeated again, then the result will be that you are completely defeated and the church cannot be manifested. You are disgusted with the sister who troubles you, and she also despises you; so how can there be the church? However, if you overcome whenever trouble comes upon you, and if you call on the name of the Lord whenever something disturbing happens to you, then even though the sisters continue to offend you, you will still love them and love the church. When you learn to live constantly in this kind of a spirit, the reality of the church is spontaneously there.

4. Experiencing Christ to Produce the Church

In the record of Matthew 16, the Lord asked the disciples, "Who do you say that I am?" Having the accurate knowledge, Peter answered, "You are the Christ, the Son of the living God." The Lord said that the vision of Him being the Christ, the Son of God, which Peter saw was correct. Then He went on to say, "I also say to you that you are Peter, and upon this rock I will build My church" (vv. 15-18). This shows us that the church life is manifested only when we realize and experience Christ. The church is not a human club or a worldly organization but an organism. When we have an inward union with the Lord and live in Him by this life union, the reality of the church is produced.

I hope that you will pray much over these points and pursue them. I have no intention of merely showing you some high visions or teaching you some truths as if you were students in a theological seminary. My burden is to help you realize and experience these visions and truths after you have seen and heard them. The way to realize and experience them is in your spirit. If you have not seen or heard these truths, you could not understand them even if you had realized them because you do not have the knowledge. Now these truths have all been completely unveiled and richly placed before you. The more you know them, the more you will realize them. The way of realization is to pray adequately to the Lord and have intimate fellowship with Him. Thus, the Lord will be the light in you, and every day you will be bright inwardly. Not one bit of shadow could remain hidden; He will correct every mistake. The law of life within you will regulate you, and you will be saved from your natural self. The last verse of *Hymns,* #501 says:

> Thy Spirit will me saturate,
> Every part will God permeate,
> Deliv'ring me from the old man,
> With all saints building for His plan.

God's building is the church. This is the practical way to experience Christ and realize the church.

5. Appreciating the Lord Jesus, Being Filled with the Spirit, and Enjoying the Father's Care for the Manifestation of the Bride

I hope that you will not just learn to know the truths but also will truly pursue to subjectively realize and experience them. I regret that when I was young, I wasted so much time. I did not waste it in pursuing entertainment, but I wasted it in studying the Bible improperly. Why do I say this? Because I did not receive the proper teaching. Those who taught me mainly taught about the "husks" and the "pods." We know that wheat needs the husks and that the peas need their pods to grow. In the same way, the Bible has some "husks" and "pods"; you do not need to get into them too much. But when I was young, I was taught to focus on these matters. I do not know how many times I studied the "seventy weeks" in Daniel 9:24-27. Yet I was never told that I have a spirit in me (Job 32:8; Zech. 12:1), that the Lord Jesus wants to abide in me (John 15:4-5), and that the Lord Jesus today is the Spirit (1 Cor. 15:45b; 2 Cor. 3:17).

Today you are surely a blessed group of people! In the Lord's recovery you are nourished, taught, and have all the riches laid out before you in a delicious, rich, and easily digestible way. Of course, you need to learn, so that your learning may help you in your understanding and enjoyment. But in particular I hope that you will be able to have a real enjoyment of the Lord in a practical way. You must live in fellowship with the Lord and abide in the Lord. We have many books among us which speak about this point, that is, that you must always contact the Lord and continuously touch Him. When you do this, you are realizing and experiencing the truths which you have heard. Today the Triune God—the Father, the Son, and the Spirit—are all in us. The more you use your spirit to contact Him and call, "O Lord Jesus," the more you will sense His supply inwardly. The more you remember Him, appreciate Him, and consider His glory, beauty, and honor, the more you will be inwardly filled with His Spirit.

The Pentecostal movement in Christianity today pays attention only to whether or not people have spoken in tongues. They always encourage people to speak in tongues; some even want people to roll around and to shout and jump. They think that this is what it means to be filled with the Holy Spirit. But the real filling by the Holy Spirit is when we inwardly appreciate and enjoy the Lord Jesus to the uttermost. The more you enjoy Him, the more you are filled with Him inwardly. Every day you need to spend some time before Him to open yourselves, to call on Him, and to appreciate Him. Then you will be filled with the Spirit inwardly. If you do not appreciate Him but still want Him to fill you, it will be impossible. This is why the experienced ones say that the more you praise the Lord Jesus, the more you will be filled with Him; it is really true. This, however, is not an outward skill. You must truly appreciate Him inwardly and from the depths of your being say, "Lord Jesus, I love You. Lord, You are exceedingly precious. It is not that I can love You, but it is because You are so lovable." If you do this, He will certainly fill you.

The main topic of Romans 1—3 is living by faith. Where does faith come from? Romans tells us that this faith is the faith in Jesus Christ or the faith of Jesus Christ (3:22). Galatians 2:20 says, "It is no longer I who live, but it is Christ who lives in me; and the life which I now live in the flesh I live in faith, the faith of the Son of God, who loved me and gave Himself up for me." Therefore, this faith is the faith of the Son of God. Faith has an object and a goal, and it is derived from that object or goal. If there were no object, how could there be faith? For example, if I were to show you a rock, you would not have any faith; on the contrary, you would be disgusted. If, however, I were to show you a big diamond, the more you look at it, the more you would have faith. This shows that faith comes from its object. The Lord Jesus is worthy of our attention. If you were to look at me, the more you look, the less faith you would have. If, however, the Lord Jesus were here, the more you look at Him, the more you would have faith. Thus, our faith comes from Him. Furthermore, our faith brings Him into us; He is one with our faith. Therefore, our faith is the faith in Him and the faith of Him.

In the same principle, we cannot be filled just by praying; unless we touch the Lord, we cannot be filled with Him. The best way to be filled by the Lord is to behold and appreciate His beauty. The more you appreciate Him, the more you will be filled by the Holy Spirit, because the Lord is the Spirit. When you appreciate and love the Lord, He enters into you and fills you as the Spirit. Furthermore, every time you touch Him, you will sense the Father's care and presence and receive the supply and transmission from the Father as the source. You will have an unutterable, indescribable enjoyment of Him. If you daily realize and experience the Triune God in this way, the reality of the church as the Body of Christ, the fullness of the One who fills all in all, will be manifested.

From the first chapter of Matthew to the last chapter of Revelation, we see this kind of vision. Matthew 1 tells us how He came into man and mingled with man. Then through the Gospels, Acts, and the Epistles to the end of Revelation, we see God, the Lamb, and the Spirit as the river of water of life proceeding out of the throne. Ultimately, the Spirit and the bride become one, speaking and announcing together. This means that the bride is full of the Spirit, full of the enjoyment of the Spirit, and that the Spirit has all the ground in her. This is God's economy. I hope that you can all pursue, realize, and experience this.

CHAPTER SEVEN

THE ACCOMPLISHMENTS OF CHRIST

(1)

Scripture Reading: John 1:3; Heb. 1:2; Luke 2:11; John 1:14, 1; Rom. 8:3; 1 Tim. 3:16; Rom. 3:25; Heb. 9:4-5; 2 Cor. 5:21; 1 Pet. 2:24; 3:18; Luke 1:35; John 6:57

OUTLINE

III. The third item of the vision—the accomplishments of Christ:
  A. Creating all things—forming the universe.
  B. Becoming flesh—bringing God into man that God and man might be joined as one.
  C. Experiencing the human life—living God among men that God may be expressed in humanity.

THE TRINITY AS THE FRAMEWORK
OF THE ENTIRE BIBLE

Before we cover the subject matter of this chapter, I would like to add a word of burden. In the Lord's recovery, particularly at the present time, all the elders, co-workers, full-timers, and serving ones must see the vision concerning the Triune God. Otherwise, the foundation of your service will be neither adequate nor firm. Sooner or later you will realize that your knowledge is just like a house built upon an insecure foundation, with one stone missing here and a cornerstone missing there. This kind of foundation will have problems sooner or later. In today's Christianity very few who serve the Lord have the vision of the Triune God as their foundation. They are afraid to talk about this matter and are also unwilling to spend time to study it. However, we must be clear that the entire Bible with sixty-six books is constructed with the Trinity.

I would like to use the building of a meeting hall as an illustration. Thirty-seven years ago I took the lead in Shanghai to build the first big meeting hall in the Lord's recovery. That meeting hall, which was located on Nanyang Road, could seat a total of five thousand. The two ends of the hall were quite far from one another. Back then, most architects did not approve of constructing a building with two ends over one hundred feet apart. This was because they felt that such a building would not be safe, since it was not possible to have beams of that length. Therefore, the design at that time was to have two supporting pillars in the middle and another two on each side. Thus, the meeting hall was divided into four sections; each section could seat one thousand two hundred fifty people, and the total seating capacity was five thousand people. If pillars were erected only on the two sides and not in the middle of the hall, the beams would not be secure.

However, when we built the meeting hall in Anaheim, the situation was altogether different. That hall is quite large—about two hundred and twenty feet long and one hundred and ten feet wide. In appearance, it is wood on top and stone at the bottom. In reality, the frame of that large meeting hall is neither wood nor stone but altogether steel. The two huge pillars at each end of the hall are steel. The beams are steel, and each beam is about one hundred and ten feet long. There are no other supporting pillars in the hall besides those on the two sides. The steel beams were made in Iowa under the supervision of the brothers, transported to Anaheim under their escort, and set up in the building also under their oversight. Furthermore, the steel beams were covered first with a layer of cement and then with a layer of stones. Therefore, when you go to the meeting hall in Anaheim, you cannot see any steel; you can only see the stones, which are for beauty, for adornment. Of course, we cannot say that the stones have no supporting strength at all; but the main strength for holding up the building lies with the steel pillars and steel beams.

By this illustration we can see clearly that the sixty-six books of the Bible are altogether built upon the Divine Trinity as their support and framework, and all the other parts are just accessories. Regretfully, Bible readers today are just like those who look at the appearance of the Anaheim meeting hall, paying attention only to whether the stones are beautiful and whether the wood is perfect. Actually, whether it is beautiful or not and whether it is perfect or not does not have any harmful effect; at least it does not endanger your life. Because the Anaheim meeting hall is supported by steel pillars, whether it seats three thousand or four thousand people, it stands there securely like a fortress or a small mountain. It cannot be affected by anything except perhaps a very great earthquake. In the same principle, the Trinity is the framework of the entire Bible, and this is especially true with the book of Ephesians in the New Testament. If you do not know the Triune God, you cannot comprehend the profoundness of Ephesians, because every chapter of this book has the Divine Trinity as its framework.

THE DIVINE TRINITY IN JOHN 14—17

The central message of the Gospel of John is found in chapters fourteen through sixteen and in the concluding prayer in chapter seventeen. What these four chapters speak about is the Divine Trinity, and their framework is the Divine

Trinity. In my youth when I attended the Sunday worship in Christianity, I heard some of the people speak about John 14. Mostly they told us that the Lord Jesus said, "I am the way and the reality and the life" (v. 6). They also said that the Lord Jesus was going away, but because He was very concerned for us, He asked the Father to give us another Comforter that He might be with us forever (v. 16), and now the Comforter has come and is taking care of us. Then others said that in chapter fifteen the Lord Jesus described the intimate relationship between Him and us by likening it to the relationship between the vine and the branches (v. 5); therefore, we should have such an intimate relationship with Him. Although they saw these things, what they saw was superficial; they did not see the Triune God as the framework.

We need to see that from the very beginning of chapter fourteen the Triune God is pointed out. The Lord said that He was going to the Father and that where He was going, the disciples knew the way. But the disciples said that they did not know the way and therefore asked Him to tell them what the way was. Then the Lord said, "I am the way and the reality and the life; no one comes to the Father except through Me" (vv. 1-6). To be "through" the Lord means to pass through the Lord. For the sake of readability, the Chinese Bible translators rendered *to the Father* as *to where the Father is,* which is not what the Greek text says. As a result, Bible readers pay attention to *where,* thinking that it denotes a place, and neglect *the Father* Himself. This is a great deviation.

Then the Lord continued His speaking, and Philip came in to interrupt Him (vv. 7-8). Philip said to Him, "Lord, show us the Father and it is sufficient for us." This means that Philip thought that he and the other disciples had been with the Lord three and a half years, yet every day they saw Him only as a Nazarene; even though the Lord had been telling them about the Father, He had never shown them the Father. Therefore, Philip asked the Lord to show them the Father, and it would be sufficient for them. Then, greatly surprised, the Lord Jesus said, "Have I been so long a time with you, and you have not known Me, Philip? He who has seen Me has seen the Father; how is it that you say, Show us the

Father? Do you not believe that I am in the Father and the Father is in Me?" (vv. 9-10). Here, the Lord presented the Son with the Father. In the Lord's speaking, the Father and the Son are inseparable because They are in each other mutually.

Then in verses 16 and 17 the Lord went on to say, "And I will ask the Father, and He will give you another Comforter, that He may be with you forever, even the Spirit of reality." The Son asked the Father to send the Spirit, and when the Spirit comes, He is not only the Comforter but also the Spirit of reality. *Comforter* is a term that is not easy to understand; few can render an accurate translation. When the British scholars were translating the Bible, they found some words that are not translatable, so they simply turned the Greek words directly into English, using them as English words. For example, *baptize* is the anglicized form of the Greek word *baptizo*. Likewise, *paraclete* is the anglicized form of the Greek word *paracletos*. This word has a variety of meanings, such as a "nurse," a "counsel," a "physician," a "nursing mother," and an "attendant." Darby said that this word has the same sense as that of the Roman "patron." A patron is one who is always beside us to meet our needs, take care of our case, and plead our cause. When the Spirit comes, He comes as such a One.

Furthermore, He is also the Spirit of reality. The Greek word for reality is *aletheia,* a word that is also very difficult to explain. It denotes something that is genuine, real, substantial, concrete. This means that although the Lord spoke so much about the Father, and although He Himself had been with the disciples for such a long time, they still could not touch Him. They had to wait until the Spirit would come to make the Father and the Son a reality in them. Therefore, the Spirit is the Spirit of reality. When the Spirit enters into the believers, the Triune God is realized in them and mingled with them to become their life and essence. This is the Triune God unveiled to us from the very beginning of John 14.

John 15 and 16 also speak about the Triune God. Both chapters fourteen and fifteen have a verse 26 that refers to the Triune God. John 14:26 says, "The Holy Spirit, whom the Father will send in My [the Son's] name"; 15:26 says, "But when the Comforter comes, whom I [the Son] will send to you from the Father, the Spirit of reality, who proceeds from the Father." Chapter fourteen says that the Father would send the Spirit in the Son's name; then chapter fifteen says that the Son would send the Spirit from the Father. The sense in Greek for the word *from* in 15:26 is "from with." This means that the Father sends the Spirit in the Son, and the Son sends the Spirit from the Father and also with the Father. Furthermore, when the Spirit comes, He comes from the Father; that is, He comes from the Father and also with the Father. And since the Father is in the Son, the Son also comes. Hence, when the Spirit comes, the Triune God comes.

These things simply cannot be described by human language; they are hard to translate and even harder to explain. Therefore, most Christians dare not touch or speak these things because they are really too difficult. What does it mean that the Father sends the Spirit in the Son? Since the Father has sent the Spirit, how is it that later the Son also sends the Spirit from the Father. Who then sends the Spirit? Is it the Father or the Son? The more we explain, the more puzzling it is. Although this truth is hard to comprehend, it becomes clear in our experience and realization.

Even when the Lord Jesus was preaching the truth on the earth, it was also hard for people to understand. In John 6 the Lord's word was so difficult to understand that many of the disciples said, "This word is hard; who can hear it?" And they went back to what they had left behind and no longer walked with Him (vv. 60, 66). Then the Lord said to the twelve, of whom Peter was the leading one, "Do you also want to go away?" Peter answered Him, "Lord, to whom shall we go? You have words of eternal life" (vv. 67-68). We see that at that time, the confused Peter was the clearest among all the others. At the end of chapter six he was very clear and not mixed up at all. How do we know? In this chapter the Lord Jesus did not use the phrase *words of eternal life;* He only said that "the words which I have spoken...are life" (v. 63). Yet Peter understood and coined the phrase *words of eternal life.* This proves that Peter was truly clear. Today some say that when we read the Bible, we should not change its words. But that day in his answer, Peter "changed" the Lord's words. When Peter heard the Lord's speaking, he realized that since the Lord's words were spirit and life, they had to be words of eternal life. Therefore, although many of the disciples did not understand what the Lord was saying, at least there was one, Peter, who understood.

Hence, I hope that, first of all, you will have a basic knowledge concerning the Divine Trinity. Then whether in the study of the Bible, in the spiritual service, or in the growth in life, you will have a foundation. Next, you must also see that our God, the Triune God in the universe, has a purpose, a plan, an intention, and a work. Since He is not a confused or mixed up God, He certainly has an economy; this is another great matter that we must see.

III. THE THIRD ITEM OF THE VISION—
THE ACCOMPLISHMENTS OF CHRIST

In this chapter and the following chapter I feel burdened to speak to you concerning another basic truth—the accomplishments of Christ. On man's side, mankind has close to six thousand years of history. On God's side, God has been existing since eternity past. What are the things accomplished by Christ in time? This is a matter that we must see.

A. Creating All Things—
Forming the Universe

According to the records of the Old and New Testaments, God made a plan and established His economy in eternity past, but then He did not do anything. It was decided that all the things that God wanted to do in His economy would be carried out by the Son. The Son came as Christ to receive the commission. The Greek word for *Christ* is *Christos,* which is the Greek translation of the Hebrew word *Messiah.* Christ was God's Messiah, God's Anointed, the One appointed by God to carry out God's commission. The Lord Jesus was not appointed after He was born as a man; rather, He had already been appointed in eternity past. In eternity past the Triune God decided that the Lord Jesus would come to accomplish everything. He was the One who would fulfill the mission of God's economy.

We must see that in the universe there are "eternity" and "time." Eternity is without beginning and without ending, whereas time has a beginning and an ending. When did time begin? It began from God's creation. When Christ created the universe and when the created things began their existence, that was the beginning of time. John 1:3 says, "All things came into being through Him, and apart from Him not one thing came into being which has come into being." *Came into being* means "came into existence." Actually, the Lord Jesus did not create from things already existing; rather, He commanded something into being out of nothing, calling the things not being as being. When He spoke, "Let there be," then all things came into being, came into existence, at once. Originally, the heavens were not there, but He said, "Let there be the heavens!" and the heavens came into existence out of nothing. In the same way the earth also came into being. All things were brought forth in this way out of nothing. Once the heavens and the earth came into existence, time began.

As God's appointed One, Christ bore the responsibility of carrying out God's commission. The first thing He accomplished was the creation of all things. Then, after the beginning of time, He went on to have many more great accomplishments. All of us who serve the Lord must see this. The purpose of His creation of all things was to bring in the universe and to form the universe. In Chinese, *universe* implies time plus space. The Hebrew expression for *universe* refers to the totality of all the ages in succession. Hebrews 1:2b says, "Through whom also He made the universe." Bible readers often come across expressions that are not so easy to understand. I believe that very few Bible readers understand the meaning of *universe;* therefore, I added a note to this verse. The definition given in this note is based upon Vincent's definition. After studying this word for a long time, I considered his definition as the best, so I excerpted it into a note in the New Testament Recovery Version. The note says, "Lit., ages. *The ages* is a Jewish expression that means *the universe. Ages* here does not refer to the matter of time but to creation (the universe) unfolded in time through successive ages." Hence, we see that the universe is composed of ages, that is, the successive ages in time.

Most Christians know that Christ created the heavens, the earth, and all things. But very few know that after His creation He is still continually forming the ages, age after age. Hence, the universe refers not only to the heavens and the earth but also to all the ages in the heavens and the earth. For example, after the creation of the heavens and the earth, Adam was created; thus, there was the age of Adam with all its stories. When the age of Adam was over, the age of Noah with its stories began. After the age of Noah, the age of Abraham with its stories occurred. When the age of Abraham was over, the age of Moses came, at which time the law was decreed. When the age of Moses was over, the age of David came. Then after all the ages of the Old Testament, there was the age of Jesus Christ, the age of the New Testament. These ages did not take place by development or evolution; rather, they were founded, instituted, by the Lord Jesus.

The Lord Jesus not only created the heavens, the earth, and all things. After creating the heavens and the earth, He instituted the ages, age after age. If there were only the heavens, the earth, and all things, without the succession of ages, then none of the stories could have happened, and there would be no universe. Hence, the universe includes not only time and space but also all the stories that happened in time and space. This is just like the scenes in a movie. In every scene the characters do not just stand still; rather, they are acting out the story according to the script. Every scene is an age. The Lord Jesus not only created the roles for us but also established the content of each scene; thus, the universe came into existence. This is the entire history of the human race.

The universe is a play with many scenes, and the Lord Jesus is not only the Director but also the Producer. The purpose of His forming the universe is to afford God the opportunity to obtain what He wants. People do not understand why a big war is going on today or why a small battle will transpire tomorrow. Many things have happened age after

age, but people in the world do not understand the mysteries
hidden in all these occurrences. Yet, these things that have
happened successively have given God the opportunity to gain
us one by one. If it were not for the changing scenes in the
world, none of us would be a Christian today. Among the
saints who are sitting here, some are from other countries
and some have a different color of skin. Yet we can use either
Chinese or English both in singing or in praying, without
much need for translation. Who can gather and blend us
together in this way? Only the Lord can.

The Lord in His sovereignty raised up the environment for
us to be saved. Some of you might not be saved if you had not
been born in Taiwan; others might not be saved if they had
not gone to America. I met some Chinese students in America
who said that when they were in Taiwan, they were not interested in the gospel and they disliked hearing about Jesus. Yet
when they went to America, they just wanted Jesus. The Lord
was not able to capture them in Taiwan, but He captured
them in America. All these things happened in the universe.
The universe creates the opportunity for God to gain what He
wants.

I very much appreciate the training here in Taiwan, in
which the East and the West are blended and have become
one family. In China forty years ago, to travel from my hometown, Chefoo, to Shanghai, one could take only the boat, and
it would take forty-eight hours. Today it takes only twelve
hours to fly from Anaheim in the United States to Taiwan.
Eighteen hours ago I made a telephone call from Taiwan to
Anaheim and told the saints who were coming to Taiwan the
things that I needed; now they have brought these things to
me. It is really convenient. This morning the ministry station
announced that while I am releasing a message here,
thirty-six places in the United States would be able to listen
in English and twenty-six places would be able to listen in
Chinese simultaneously. I hope that one day we will be able to
transmit by man-made satellites. Then the messages that are
released here can be simultaneously heard in Japan, Indone-
sia, and other places. This is the way we will take so that the
messages that are being released in one place can be heard at

the same time throughout the whole earth. All these things belong to the realm of the "universe" accomplished by Christ.

B. Becoming Flesh—
Bringing God into Man That God and Man Might Be Joined as One

God created the heavens and the earth and then He created Adam. Then four thousand years later, God became flesh. Today most Christians rarely hear the truth concerning God's incarnation. Mostly they just sing some Christmas carols or announce the good news on Christmas Eve. Although they have a very good hymn (*Hymns,* #84) written by Charles Wesley concerning the birth of Christ, there is not one place in that hymn that definitely and solemnly tells people that, through His birth, the Lord Jesus brought God into man that God and man may be joined as one. It mainly tells us that an angel announced the good news, saying, "Today a Savior has been born to you in David's city, who is Christ the Lord" (Luke 2:11).

The angel's announcement of the good news is recorded in the Gospel of Luke, telling us that the Lord Jesus was born to be a Savior. But the Gospel of John does not announce the glad tidings of the Savior's birth; rather, it says, "The Word became flesh" (1:14). This is the good news in the Gospel of John. The Word became flesh, and this Word was God (v. 1), not just a partial God, but the entire God, including the Father, the Son, and the Spirit. The Word was God, and this God became flesh. This is the amazing good news. This good news is not just that the Savior, Christ, was born to us, but it is that God became flesh. If this word were not in the Bible, and if it were merely my own speaking, I am afraid that none of you would believe it.

"The Word became flesh" is not a sweet expression. According to the fact, it is sweet, but according to the word *flesh,* it is not sweet. Yet, who was Christ? Christ was God becoming flesh. Who was the One who was born? The One who was born was God who entered into man that divinity and humanity might be united, and not only united but mingled together to become one entity, one person. He is a person, yet within this person are two natures, not only joined but mingled together.

Today in Christianity there is still a great heresy that opposes the truth concerning mingling. I pointed out in the book *Concerning the Person of Christ* that in the first few centuries a heretical group advocated that when divinity and humanity were mingled, the two natures merged into one and became a third nature. This has stirred up those who oppose the truth concerning mingling, even to the present time. I also referred to the type of mingling in the Old Testament, that is, oil being mingled with fine flour to make the unleavened cakes to be offered to God (Lev. 2). Bible readers know that oil denotes the divine nature, while fine flour denotes the human nature. When oil and fine flour are mingled, each still retains its own characteristics, yet they are mingled to become one entity, the unleavened cake. Hence, the unleavened cake is one entity with two natures; both natures still exist, yet they are mingled together, without a third nature being produced. This marvelous thing typifies the mingling of divinity with humanity. We must see that after we are saved, God has come into us not only to be joined but also to be mingled with us.

Perhaps some will say that the Bible tells us that Christ Jesus came into the world to save sinners (1 Tim. 1:15) and that God sent His Son to be the propitiation for our sins (Rom. 3:25; 1 John 2:2; 4:10). The Bible indeed says these things, but Christ's becoming the propitiation to save sinners is a procedure to reach the goal, which is for God to enter into man. In order to enter into man, God must remove the obstacles between Him and man. The first obstacle is sin; hence, sin must be removed. Otherwise, God cannot enter into man. Hence, God became flesh, and with the flesh and in the flesh He became the offerings (cf. Heb. 10:5-10), such as the sin offering (2 Cor. 5:21; Rom. 8:3) and the trespass offering (1 Pet. 2:24; 3:18) as sacrifices of propitiation to completely remove the most serious obstacle between God and man. Thus, God can enter into man to be joined and even mingled with man. This is His greatest accomplishment through incarnation.

C. Experiencing the Human Life—
Living God among Men
That God May Be Expressed in Humanity

The Lord Jesus did not go to die on the cross with His flesh immediately after His incarnation. Instead, He lived the human life for thirty-three and a half years on the earth. The four Gospels show us that the Lord lived out God in His humanity when He was in the process of experiencing the human life. While He was living out God, He did not make it known, saying, "Behold, here comes God! When I come, God comes." Rather, He lived out God in His living that people might see God. The main thing He did in His thirty-three and a half years of living on the earth was to live out God. He did not bring God out for people to see. Instead, He simply lived out God in His humanity. What He lived out always had the element of humanity, yet that humanity was full of divinity. He lived out human virtues, yet every virtue incorporated a divine attribute. The divine attributes were lived out in His human virtues. When He loved people, you may say that was man's love, or you may also say that was God's love shown in man's love. In any case, that was God's love and that was God expressed in Jesus' humanity. He lived such a life of the mingling of God with man for thirty-three and a half years.

Today most Bible readers only see the miracles in the Gospels, such as the blind receiving sight, the lame walking, the lepers being cleansed, the deaf hearing, and the dead being raised (Luke 7:22). They have not seen that these four biographies are a portrayal of a man who passed through human life to live out another life. The Lord Himself clearly said, "As the living Father has sent Me and I live because of the Father" (John 6:57a). This means that although the Lord was a man, He lived out God's life and not His own life. As a result, God and He, He and God, had one life and one living; They both lived by the same life and lived out the same living. This is such a marvelous thing that it cannot be expressed even by the relationship between husband and wife. We must have a clear realization concerning this matter. We need to know that after we have been saved, we should be such persons living such a life. After saying that He lived because of the Father, the Lord went on to say, "So he who eats Me, he also shall live because of Me" (v. 57b). Just as He lived out God's life, so we should likewise live out His life. Just as He had one life and one living with God, so we also should have one life and one living with Him. This is the truth in the Bible.

The truth in the Bible is not meant to improve you. It is meant only to work the Triune God into you to be your life and living. The thirty-three and a half years of human living of the Lord Jesus on earth are a pattern and a model. According to our experience, after being saved we often feel that the life we live is indescribable because it is a living of God mingled with man in which God and man have one life and one living. We should live this kind of life every day. It seems that the New Testament contains some words for improvement, words that teach us to reform ourselves and to do good. However, if we study the context carefully, we will see that those are the fruits of our having the same life and the same living with Christ our Lord. We all must see this.

In His experience of the human life the Lord Jesus lived out God among men that God might be expressed in humanity. I hope that you all can see and be controlled by this vision. Thus, you will know the meaning and the goal of your pursuit for the growth in life and your endeavor in the spiritual service. The goal of our pursuing is to allow God to be lived out through us that we and He may have one life and one living and also to allow Him to express His divine attributes through our human virtues. These are the words in the Bible with the most intrinsic life element. I hope that you can see this clearly. Furthermore, I hope that you will look up the relevant Scripture verses, studying and digesting them carefully, and then apply, pursue, and learn them practically in your living.

CHAPTER EIGHT

THE ACCOMPLISHMENTS OF CHRIST

(2)

Scripture Reading: Gen. 3:15, 21; Isa. 53:7; Dan. 9:25-26; Zech. 12:10; John 8:44; 1:29; Rom. 8:3; Matt. 1:21; Heb. 9:28a; 1 Pet. 2:24; John 3:14; Heb. 2:14b; John 12:31; Gal. 6:14a; 1 Cor. 15:45b; Rom. 6:6; Gal. 2:20; 6:14b; Col. 1:15b, 20; Eph. 2:14-16; John 12:24; Rev. 13:8

OUTLINE

D. Passing through death—dealing with sin, Satan, the world, the flesh, the old man, and the old creation with its ordinances and releasing the divine life to accomplish redemption:
1. The types, prophecies, and fulfillment in the Bible.
2. The death of Christ dealing with sin, Satan, the world, the flesh, the old man, and the old creation with its ordinances and releasing the divine life:
   a. Dealing with sin:
      1) Sin and sins.
      2) The source of sin—the devil's private possession.
      3) The dealing of sin—the inward sin and the outward sins.
   b. Dealing with Satan.
   c. Dealing with the world.
   d. Dealing with the flesh.
   e. Dealing with the old man.

f. Dealing with the old creation.

g. Dealing with ordinances.

h. Releasing the divine life.

3. Our experience and application.

The truths concerning the accomplishments of Christ have been made shallow by the majority of today's Christian teachers. Perhaps some will say that Christianity also preaches the gospel and speaks about the Lord Jesus' crucifixion, shedding of blood, forgiveness of sins, and accomplishment of redemption, as well as His resurrection and ascension. It is true that the fundamentalists speak about all these matters, but what they speak is very shallow and too common. As a result, these shallow, common things occupy people's inner being and hinder them from receiving the deeper truths. If you talk to Christians about what the Bible teaches concerning Christ's death, resurrection, and ascension, you will discover that they have no ear or heart to hear. This proves that the taste within them has been spoiled so that they have no ear to hear. Mothers know that they should not give just any kind of food to their children; otherwise, they will spoil their children's taste, and their children will not take the proper, nutritious food. Many truths taught in Christianity are just candies; they are not only shallow but also damaging to people's taste.

On the other hand, I hope that you will change your concept. Do not be so proud to think that you know everything. The main revelation of the New Testament is the three accomplishments of Christ: His death, His resurrection, and His ascension. This is not to say that His incarnation and His human living are insignificant. They are also profound but easier to explain. The death of Christ is not only profound but also hard to preach because it involves many complicated items and includes many details. The same is true with His resurrection and ascension.

D. Passing through Death—Dealing with Sin, Satan, the World, the Flesh, the Old Man, and the Old Creation with Its Ordinances and Releasing the Divine Life to Accomplish Redemption

Concerning the accomplishments of Christ, we have already covered three items: creating all things, becoming flesh, and passing through human life. Now we will go on to consider the fourth point: passing through death—dealing with sin, Satan, the world, the flesh, the old man, and the old creation with its ordinances and releasing the divine life to accomplish redemption.

1. The Types, Prophecies, and Fulfillment in the Bible

The matter of the death of the Lord Jesus is covered in the New Testament from the Gospels to Revelation. The Old Testament also contains many types and prophecies concerning this matter. The first type, which is also a prophecy, is the seed of the woman. This is recorded in Genesis 3:15, where God said to the serpent, "He [the seed of the woman] will bruise you on the head, / But you will bruise him on the heel." This refers to the death of Christ. Although we cannot see the word *death* here, it indeed implies the death of Christ. Furthermore, after their transgression, Adam and Eve immediately had the consciousness of sin and were ashamed of their nakedness, so they sewed fig leaves together and made loincloths for themselves. What they did, however, was according to their own way and was ineffective. Therefore, God made them coats of skins for their covering (vv. 6-7, 21). We know that skins imply a great deal. Skins were taken from oxen or sheep. Before the skins were taken, the oxen or sheep had to die. Therefore, skins imply death. The oxen or sheep had to be killed before their skins could be made into clothing to cover man's shame. This shows us a type of the substituting death, the death that covers man's sin.

Then we go on to chapter four, where the Bible says that Cain presented an offering to God from the fruit of the ground (v. 3). There was no shedding of blood with the fruit of the ground because it did not pass through death. Abel, however, presented an offering from the firstlings of his flock, that is, from their fat portions; in this we can see death. The lamb sacrificed by Abel typifies Christ, who as the Lamb of God (John 1:29) was slain on the cross by the righteous God and who through death shed His precious blood to redeem us (1 Pet. 1:18-19) and to cover us with Himself as our righteousness (cf. Luke 15:22). Here it is implied that a sacrifice was slain and blood was shed; this typifies Christ's death. Hence, we can see everywhere in the Bible the matter concerning the death of Christ.

Let us cite three prophecies in the Old Testament concerning the death of Christ. First, Isaiah 53:7 says, "Like a lamb that is led to the slaughter / And like a sheep that is dumb before its shearers, / So He did not open His mouth." Second, Daniel 9:25-26 says, "From the issuing of the decree to restore and rebuild Jerusalem until the time of Messiah the Prince will be seven weeks and sixty-two weeks....And after the sixty-two weeks Messiah will be cut off." This tells us that the year of Christ's death would be the seventh year of the sixty-ninth week. Third, Zechariah 12:10 says, "And I will pour out on the house of David and on the inhabitants of Jerusalem the Spirit of grace and of supplications; and they will look upon Me, whom they have pierced." Then 13:6 says, "And someone will say to Him, What are these wounds between Your arms? And He will say, Those with which I was wounded in the house of those who love Me." The One "whom they have pierced" is Christ, and the "wounds between [His] arms" denote the spear wound He suffered on the cross (John 19:34). All these are prophecies concerning Christ's death.

The New Testament is filled even more with words concerning the death of Christ. For example, Romans 8:3 says, "God, sending His own Son in the likeness of the flesh of sin and concerning sin, condemned sin in the flesh." Paul did not directly mention the death of Christ; instead, he said "condemned sin." To condemn sin is to judge sin. This judgment is not carried out before the judgment seat but in the death of Christ on the cross. This implies Christ's death. By these illustrations you can realize that many passages in the Bible refer to the death of Christ.

2. The Death of Christ Dealing with Sin, Satan, the World, the Flesh, the Old Man, and the Old Creation with Its Ordinances and Releasing the Divine Life

Now we will go on to see how the death of Christ dealt with all the negative persons, matters, and things in the universe, such as Satan, the world, sin, the flesh, the old man, the old creation with all its ordinances and all persons, matters, and things involved. We will also see the positive aspect of Christ's death in releasing the divine life. The dealing by the death of Christ is all-inclusive. All the negative persons, matters, and things in the universe were dealt with in the death of Christ.

a. Dealing with Sin

The Lord Jesus died on the cross firstly to deal with sin. The matter of sin involves a great deal. In Chinese theology, two terms are used concerning sin: *yuan tsui* (original sin) and *pen tsui* (one's own sin). Because *yuan* and *pen* in Chinese are synonymous, I often mixed up these two terms when I was young. *Yuan tsui,* the original sin, refers to the sin committed by Adam; whereas *pen tsui,* one's own sin, refers to sins committed by ourselves. Adam is the forefather of the human race, so the sin he committed is *yuan tsui,* the original sin. The sins we committed ourselves are *pen tsui,* our own sins. In another sense, the original sin is the nature of sin, whereas the sins we committed ourselves are the deeds of sin. Furthermore, the original sin is sin itself, whereas our own sins are the fruits of sin. To use modern expressions, the original sin is the "sin-gene," whereas our own sins are the outcome of sin. Actually, this kind of saying is still not accurate enough.

1) Sin and Sins

Brother Nee pointed out that, according to Darby's study of the New Testament, sins (plural) are dealt with in Romans 1:1 through 5:11 and beginning with 5:12 sin (singular) is dealt with. Sin is inward and is related to our nature; sins are outward and are related to our position. The Lord Jesus' death on the cross dealt primarily not with sins but with sin, the gene of sin.

Sins are the outcome of sin, the descendants of sin; they are not sin itself. For example, Isaiah 53:6b says, "And Jehovah has caused the iniquity of us all / To fall on Him." "Iniquity" here is an offspring of sin. Sin has many offsprings, such as transgressions, iniquities (v. 5), sins of guilt (Psa. 69:5), errors (19:12), turning aside (Deut. 17:17), wickedness, and trespasses. All of these are fruits born of sin. Also, Hebrews 9:28 says, "So Christ also, having been offered once to bear the sins of many, will appear a second time to those who eagerly await Him, apart from sin, unto salvation." In this verse, first there is *sins* (plural), and then there is *sin* (singular). We can understand this only by a careful study.

Sin has a function, and it is called a "law," the law of sin (Rom. 7:23, 25). How does this law operate? Whenever it operates, man commits sins. This law does not know how to do good, it cannot do good, and its expertise is not to do good. As soon as it begins to operate, man begins to commit sins; this is the law of sin. Today people have discovered many laws; but two thousand years ago, when science was not yet so advanced, Paul had already discovered four laws, one of which was the law of sin. The Chinese philosophers discovered this law a little later, but instead of calling it a law, they called it a "principle."

The law of sin is the automatic function of sin itself; it is also the natural power of sin. When sin lies dormant, the law remains inactive. But once sin becomes active, the law of sin begins to work; consequently, man commits sins. Paul said that the evil was present with him whenever he wanted to do good (v. 21) and that he did not do the good which he wanted to do, but the evil which he did not want to do, that he practiced (v. 19). Therefore, he found out that the law of sin was with him when he wanted to do good. This proves that in him there was something which was called "sin." This thing has a spontaneous function. When it is asleep, there is no problem, but once it is aroused, terrible things happen. In Romans 7 Paul said that the function of the law was to awaken the law of sin which was asleep in him (v. 9). When the law shouted, sin was awakened; when sin became active, the law of sin began to operate. Consequently, he sinned. Here, Paul was speaking about the sin itself, the "sin-gene," and not the issue, the fruit, of sin.

2) The Source of Sin—the Devil's Private Possession

In John 8:44 the Lord Jesus said to the Jews, "You are of

your father the devil....He was a murderer from the beginning....When he speaks the lie, he speaks it out of his own
possessions." This is the proper translation according to the
Greek text. The Chinese Union Version translates it this way:
"When he speaks the lie, he speaks out of himself." Lü Chen-
chung's Version translates it another way: "When he speaks
the lie, he speaks out of his own nature." Both are not the
meaning of what the Lord Jesus expressed at that time. The
Lord Jesus' speaking was full of wisdom. In describing
the relationship between Satan and sin, He said that sin is
something of Satan's own. Greek experts affirm that this
expression denotes something which Satan has within himself, something as Satan's private possession, something as a
secret in him. Hence, the Lord Jesus' word means that the
devil lies out of his private possession, which is the source of
lies.

Up to the present we still cannot explain what Satan's
private possession is. However, by the word of the Lord Jesus
we can be sure that this private possession of the devil is the
source of sin. Because of this, Satan has a name which is called
"the evil." Within Satan there is an evil thing that is not
found in any other angel or any other creature; it is uniquely
his. If you ask me what this evil thing is, then I would tell you
that this evil thing which uniquely belongs to Satan is called
"sin" in the Bible. Then if you ask me further where sin came
from, I can only tell you that although many have been trying
to find out where sin came from, it is still a secret. Even the
Chinese philosophers who achieved a great deal in their
study concerning the origin of sin were unable to answer this
question.

Nevertheless, the Bible impresses us deeply with the fact
that sin is Satan's private possession, something of Satan's
own, something that is uniquely and exclusively his. Therefore, he is the father of liars and the father of lies. Not only
the liars are of him, but even the lies are essentially of him.
There is something within him as his private possession, and
this is the gene of sin. When he seduced Eve and Adam by
instigating them to eat the fruit of the tree of the knowledge
of good and evil, the gene of sin entered into man. This is why

Romans 5:12 says, "Therefore just as through one man sin entered into the world." *World* here denotes the people of the world. It is the same as the word for *world* in John 3:16, which says "For God so loved the world." This is the way sin entered into man.

Therefore, strictly speaking, the understanding of the early Chinese theologians concerning sin was not quite accurate. They considered *yuan tsui,* the original sin, as the sin committed by our forefather Adam, and *pen tsui,* our own sin, as the sins committed by ourselves. Actually, the original sin is not the sin committed by Adam. The sin committed by Adam, to Adam himself, was Adam's own sin. The original sin is something of Satan's own, something as Satan's private possession. This is the origin, the source, of sin.

3) The Dealing of Sin— the Inward Sin and the Outward Sins

What the Lord Jesus dealt with on the cross was sin, the sin itself. This is why, after Romans 7, Paul said in 8:3, "God, sending His own Son in the likeness of the flesh of sin and concerning sin, condemned sin in the flesh." This means that there is something called sin, and when the Lord Jesus was crucified, sin was also crucified. In this way God judged sin in the flesh of the Lord Jesus. Furthermore, God condemned sin by sending His Son "in the likeness of the flesh of sin" and also "concerning sin." *Concerning sin* means including anything that is related to sin.

Although this One whom God sent was "in the likeness of the flesh of sin," there was no sin in Him (2 Cor. 5:21; Heb. 4:15). This is typified by the bronze serpent which Moses lifted up in the wilderness (Num. 21:9). In John 3:14 the Lord Jesus said, "And as Moses lifted up the serpent in the wilderness, so must the Son of Man be lifted up." This word indicates that the bronze serpent was a type of Him as our Substitute on the cross. The bronze serpent had the form of the serpent but was without the serpent's poison; it had the serpent's form but not the serpentine nature. When the bronze serpent was hung on the pole, only the serpent's form was hung there; it was not an actual poisonous serpent. In the same principle, when the Lord Jesus was put to death on the cross, He was crucified in the flesh; that flesh was "the likeness of the flesh of sin," the form of sin. It was in such a "likeness of the flesh of sin" that God condemned sin and dealt with everything related to sin.

Not only so, since man has the gene of sin within, he surely has the deeds of sin without. The Lord Jesus dealt with our inward sin, the gene of sin, by becoming sin on our behalf and condemning and judging sin in the flesh of sin. He dealt with our outward sins by bearing our sins and suffering God's righteous punishment on our behalf to satisfy God's righteous requirement. This is Christ's passing through death to deal with our sins. This is proven by Isaiah 53:6, Hebrews 9:28, and 1 Peter 2:24.

b. Dealing with Satan

Today the kingdom of Satan consists of three categories of beings: one category comprises the rebellious, fallen angels in the air as the messengers of Satan; another category comprises the demons in the water; and still another category comprises the fallen human beings on earth. The fallen angels include "the authority of the air" mentioned in Ephesians 2:2 and "the rulers," "the authorities," "the world-rulers of this darkness," and "the spiritual forces of evil in the heavenlies" mentioned in 6:12. The rulers and authorities of the air are the messengers under Satan. Originally, in the preadamic universe, God entrusted the angels with the ruling authority (cf. Heb. 2:5; Rev. 4:4, 10). When Satan rebelled against God, some of the angels followed Satan in his rebellion (12:4, 9) and became the fallen angels, the unclean spirits. The demons are some of the living creatures who lived on the earth in the preadamic age and were judged by God when they joined Satan's rebellion (Job 9:4-7); thus, they lost their bodies and became the disembodied spirits, who are restricted to the waters (Gen. 1:2; cf. Rev. 20:13) and need human bodies as a means to carry out their activities on the earth. Therefore, sometimes they intentionally cling to the human body. Since these unclean spirits, the demons, are related to Satan, they

were all judged and dealt with by God through the crucifixion
of the Lord Jesus (John 3:14; Heb. 2:14b).

c. Dealing with the World

On the cross the Lord also judged the world and cast out
Satan, the ruler of the world (John 12:31). The Greek word for
world is *kosmos,* denoting "an order," "a set form," "an orderly
arrangement," hence, an ordered system set up by Satan, the
adversary of God. All the things on the earth, especially those
related to mankind, such as religion, culture, education, in-
dustry, and commerce, and all the things in the air have been
systematized by Satan into his kingdom of darkness to form
an anti-God world system on the earth. This whole satanic
system lies in the evil one (1 John 5:19).

Besides *kosmos,* the Bible uses another Greek word, *aion,*
with reference to the world. *Aion* means an "age," "era," and it
denotes the modern appearance or the fashion of the world.
Every age has its modern appearance, its fashion, its customs
(cf. Eph. 2:2); it is the actual world encountered by people and
it includes "the things in the world" (1 John 2:15). This shows
us the difference between *kosmos,* the world, and *aion,* an age.
Kosmos refers to the entire world, whereas *aion* refers to
an age as a part of the world. The entire world from the past
to the future is a *kosmos,* a whole entity, composed of many
ages, each of which is an *aion.* Hence, *world* is a general term,
whereas *age* is a specific term.

The world involves all persons, things, and matters as well
as all the ages. Every age has its fashion. For example, the
time prior to the Ching Dynasty was an age, and the people at
that time had their fashion. Then, after the Republic was
established, that was the age of the Republic, and the people
at that time had their fashion. But today, to us, those things
have become ancient, antique, and are no longer fashionable.
I still remember forty-four years ago while I was preaching
the gospel in Chefoo, a very modern lady attended the meetings. She grew up in my hometown but was educated in
Shanghai. When she came to listen to the gospel, she had her
hair up in four layers. When she walked in, I felt uncomfort-
able looking at her. After a few times when she came again,

one layer of her hair was gone; then soon afterwards, another layer was gone; eventually, all the layers were completely torn down. I felt very happy because it proved the effectiveness of the gospel.

The world involves a great number of items, including all the ages. The ages have all been systematized by Satan to usurp and frustrate man from fulfilling the purpose of God and distract man from the enjoyment of God. When Satan, the ruler of this world, was cast out through the crucifixion of the Lord in His flesh, the evil system, the kingdom of darkness, was also judged. Hence, the death of Christ also dealt with the world.

d. Dealing with the Flesh

Genesis 6:3 says, "And Jehovah said, My Spirit will not strive with man forever, for he indeed is flesh." Man's body was transmuted into flesh because the element of the tree of the knowledge of good and evil, the element of Satan, was added into it (3:7). In the Bible the flesh includes man's corrupted body (Rom. 6:6; 7:24), the entire fallen man (3:20; Gal. 2:16), and even the good aspects of man (Phil. 3:3-6). Everything, whether good or bad, is of the flesh as long as it is of ourselves. In Romans 8:8, concerning the flesh Paul made this conclusion: "And those who are in the flesh cannot please God." The greatest reason that God abhors the flesh so much is that Satan dwells in the flesh. The flesh is the headquarters of God's enemy, the largest base of the operation of God's enemy. We may say that all the works that Satan carries out in man are based on man's flesh. Therefore, God hates the flesh just as much as He hates Satan; God wants to destroy the flesh just as much as He wants to destroy Satan. Through His becoming a man in the flesh (John 1:14) and dying in the form of the fallen man and in the likeness of the flesh of sin (Rom. 8:3), Christ dealt with the fallen flesh.

e. Dealing with the Old Man

In the old creation we are the old man. The old man is lived out in the flesh and is inclined to keep the law. When we were the old man, the old husband, we were under the bondage of the law. Whatever we were or whatever we did was unto death (7:4-5). However, Christ has come, and the old man has been crucified with Him as the last Adam (1 Cor. 15:45b; Rom. 6:6; Gal. 2:20; 6:14b). Since the old man has been crucified, the regenerated man is now free from the law of the old man (Rom. 7:3-4, 6; Gal. 2:19); hence, we are no longer under the law but under grace that we may live to God.

f. Dealing with the Old Creation

As the Firstborn of all creation (Col. 1:15b), Christ died on the cross in the old creation, and through such a death He terminated the entire old creation and accomplished redemption for all creation. The entire old creation is typified by the cherubim on the riven veil in the temple (Exo. 26:31; Ezek. 1:5, 10; 10:14-15; Matt. 27:51). Luke 23:44-45 says, "And it was now about the sixth hour, and darkness fell over the whole land until the ninth hour, the sun's light failing; and the veil of the temple was split down the middle." Darkness here is related to sin, whereas the veil typifies the flesh of the Lord Jesus, because Hebrews 10:20 refers to "a new and living way through the veil, that is, His flesh." The cherubim embroidered on the veil which was split at the Lord Jesus' death represent all creation. This means that when Christ died in the flesh, He brought all creation with Him. When the veil in the temple was split, the cherubim embroidered on the veil were also split. This indicates that when Christ was crucified in the flesh, all the creatures were crucified with Him. Through this, all the created things, whether the things on the earth or the things in the heavens, were reconciled to God (Col. 1:20). Therefore, Hebrews 2:9 clearly says that Christ tasted death not only on behalf of everyone but also on behalf of everything.

g. Dealing with Ordinances

By passing through death Christ dealt with sin, Satan, the world, the flesh, the old man, and the old creation. Furthermore, His death was also for the creation of the one new man. In order to create the one new man, Christ had to abolish all the ordinances and all the different customs of living, habits, traditions, and practices among human beings. Thus, as the Peacemaker Christ created all His believers, both Jews and Gentiles, in Himself into one new man (Eph. 2:14-16). Not only are there barriers between the Jews and the Gentiles, but there are also barriers among the nationalities and races. Unless these barriers are removed, we cannot be one in Christ as the new man. Praise the Lord, on the cross Christ has abolished all the ordinances! Now in the church life, regardless of our race, color, nationality, status, and habits of living, we can be built together to become the Body of Christ as one new man.

h. Releasing the Divine Life

All the negative persons, things, and matters in the universe, including sin, Satan, the world, the flesh, the old man, the entire creation, and the ordinances were dealt with through the death of Christ. On the positive side, as the grain of wheat falling into the ground and dying, Christ released the divine life (John 12:24) and imparted it into us so that, like Him, we may become many grains to be made into one bread as His Body (1 Cor. 10:17a). Thus, He accomplished an all-inclusive death.

3. Our Experience and Application

Since the Lord Jesus dealt with sin on the cross, is sin still in us today? Is sin alive or dead in us today? And how about the law of sin now? We all must admit that sin is still one of our biggest problems. Furthermore, the Lord also dealt with the old man on the cross, but is our old man truly dead? Hebrews 2:14 says that the Lord destroyed the devil through death. This is a fulfillment of the prophecy in Genesis 3:15 concerning bruising the serpent's head. However, is the devil alive or dead today? It is true that these were all dealt with in the all-inclusive death of the Lord Jesus, but in our feelings and our practical experiences, sin still lives, the old man also still lives, and the devil lives even more.

On the surface, it seems that the Bible contradicts itself. On the one hand, Hebrews 2:14 says that the Lord Jesus partook of blood and flesh and destroyed Satan through His death on the cross. But Paul, who wrote Hebrews, also told us to beware of the devil lest we be taken advantage of by him, for we are not ignorant of his schemes (2 Cor. 2:11). In Ephesians 6:11 Paul also exhorted us to put on the whole armor of God that we may be able to stand against the stratagems of the devil. If Paul were here, perhaps someone would ask him how he could reconcile his words. Furthermore, at the end of the Bible, in Revelation 20:1-3, there is a strong angel coming with a great chain in his hand to lay hold of Satan, bind him for a thousand years, and cast him into the abyss. If Satan was already dead, why would there still be the need to bind him? And after one thousand years, he will then be released again to deceive the nations in the four corners of the earth (vv. 7-8). That will be his final activity, in which he would deceive the nations on the earth to rebel against God for the last time. According to these records, has Satan, the devil, been dealt with?

We must realize that the revelations in the Bible always have two sides: one side is the fact and the other side is the fulfillment. Likewise, we need two kinds of seeing: one kind is the actual seeing and the other kind is the seeing by faith. The actual seeing is the seeing according to what we actually feel. According to this kind of seeing, Satan is not dead, our old man is not dead, and the sin in us is not dead. But according to the seeing by faith, that is, according to God's view, all these items which we see as alive are already actually dead. This may be illustrated by the fact that although the Lord Jesus was crucified two thousand years ago, in God's eyes He had already been crucified from the foundation of the world (13:8).

The reason that the Bible gives us revelations is to produce faith in us that we may have the seeing of faith. Faith is not something which we have naturally; faith is produced by seeing certain persons, things, and matters which we appreciate. For example, when you see a piece of clay, you do not treasure it in your heart and therefore you do not have faith in it; instead, you reject it. However, when you see a diamond, you appreciate it in your heart and thus faith is spontaneously produced. Thus, the book of Revelation shows us a treasure, and because we appreciate it, faith is produced in us. On the one hand, faith is not by sight; on the other hand, faith greatly requires seeing, that is, it requires revelation. The Bible is full of revelations, and even the last book is called Revelation, a book that reveals the treasures. Therefore, today when we read the Bible, we need to learn not only to read the dead letter but even more to see the revelations contained therein. Once we see the revelation, faith will spontaneously be produced in us. Once we have faith, we are living in the vision, and as a result, our old man, sin, and the devil will all be dead in our experience. However, if we do not live in the vision which Revelation has shown us, our old man, sin, and the devil will all be alive.

We must realize that all persons, things, and matters are false and that only God and His words are real. While we are living on the earth, we must believe only in God and in His words and not in the environment that we see. This means that we must believe in God's view and not in our actual view. We have to declare: "It is a lie that Satan lives! It is a lie that sin lives! And it is a lie that our old man lives!" This is because, according to God's view, actually all these items have already died. However, this requires us first to have a revelation, a vision, to see that they are all dead, and then to make the declaration in faith. Vision is the scene shown to us by God's revelation; our faith is produced from the seeing of the vision. As a result, we acknowledge and experience what God has revealed to us.

Today we are here not just to study the doctrines in letter, nor are we here conducting a seminary. What we are doing is to dig out the treasures that are buried underneath the letter of the Bible and to show them to you for your realization. In God's eyes all the negative things in the universe have already died. Satan has died, sin has died, and our old man has died. These are accomplished facts in the eyes of God. Revelation is a book completely of prophecies. According to the nature of prophecies, the verbs used should be in the future tense. But the strange thing is that nearly all the verbs in Revelation are in the past tense, indicating that all the things referred to in the book have all been accomplished. This means that God sees all those things as things that have already been accomplished. Those who have the vision will say, "Amen!" Where are we today? If you see according to God's view, you will say, "I am not in the city of Taipei; rather, I am in the holy city, New Jerusalem!" This is because in God's eyes we are in the New Jerusalem now. However, when those who are without a vision read the book of Revelation, they think that it is still too early to enter into the New Jerusalem, since Paul and John have been waiting for two thousand years and have not yet entered. Therefore, they consider that the New Jerusalem is something that will take place a long time from now. Actually, in faith, we are already in the New Jerusalem.

Sin, Satan, and the old man are already dead! We should have this vision and declare in faith: "Already dead! Already dealt with!" The key is in what you believe. If you believe that it is dead, then it is dead; if you do not believe that it is dead, then it is not dead. The Bible is a covenant, including the old covenant and the new covenant. The fulfillment of a covenant is conditional. The condition for the old covenant is the law, whereas the condition for the new covenant is faith. This is why many places in the New Testament mention faith (Eph. 4:5, 13; 1 Tim. 1:4; Titus 1:4; 2 Pet. 1:1; Jude 3). But how can we have faith? In illustration, there are many jewelry stores in Hong Kong. When you go to visit any jewelry store, the owner will not only ask you verbally to buy the gems, but even more he will also display the gems before your eyes. Once you see them, you have faith. The entire Bible, especially the New Testament, is a revelation that shows us the facts according to God's view. When you see it, you have faith.

Today many Christians have not seen these treasures, so they show people only "stones and clay." Consequently, the more they preach, the more people do not believe. But when we preach, we need only fifteen minutes to get people saved. This is because we show them the treasures instead of speaking to them about such superficial matters as going to heaven or going to hell. When they see the treasures, they will believe and desire to receive salvation. The way to be saved is to repent (Matt. 4:17), to call (Rom. 10:13), and to believe into (John 1:12-13), which is to receive. When we receive, we obtain salvation. This is exactly our practice.

What is covered in this chapter is a great vision and a great deliverance. I hope that you all could see, receive, and enter into it. For example, concerning the truth about sin, you need to find all the verses in the New Testament that mention sin (singular) and then study them and pray over them, asking the Lord to give you the vision. Then you will realize that sin has already been crucified and it has been condemned by God. Then you will be able to thank and praise the Lord, and you will have faith. Likewise, concerning Satan, the world, and the old man, as you see each item, you receive it and obtain it. Then what you learn is real, thorough, and subjective.

CHAPTER NINE

AN EVALUATION OF
THE PRACTICE OF THE NEW WAY

(1)

In this and the following chapter, we review the practice of the new way so that we may make some changes and adjustments. This may be likened to the need of examining the Passover lamb before it could be offered. Our purpose in doing this is not to find fault but to make a proper assessment.

THE NEED FOR STUDY AND ADJUSTMENT

Since October of 1984 we have brought up the matter of changing the system. At that time I called together the saints in the church in Taipei and told them that our changing of the system is to discard the old practices of the past and adopt new practices for doing everything. The so-called new practices are those which are already in the holy Scriptures but are not being practiced by us. We have been practicing the old way with ease, and now all of a sudden we want to practice the new way, and the so-called new way has not yet been paved. Therefore, we need to continue probing as we go along, researching on the one hand and adjusting on the other. At the same time, I also told the saints that although I vigorously brought up the matter of changing the system, I myself did not have any confidence. This is because although I had experienced and had gotten into many things, I had not yet done any research on how to practice the new way, and neither had I personally experienced it. For this reason we are studying while we are practicing; no final conclusion has been made.

Any matter without a final conclusion is very difficult

to carry out, and complications can easily arise. Generally, Christians have the religious concept that people must worship in a big chapel to be proper. Today in the research stage of our practice of the new way, we must at least get rid of this kind of religious formality. On the positive side, however, we still have to improve.

An Example of a Home Meeting

Last Saturday I attended a meeting in a home. If I had not gone, no one would have been baptized, but I went, and two persons were baptized. In that home meeting there were many gospel friends, and they were very open. Some of them had been to the meeting many times already, and one of them even helped in serving. But the meeting had gone on for a long time, and still no one was going to be baptized. I refrained, however, from doing anything right away; rather, I yielded the meeting to the saints. I wanted to understand why they had so many good gospel candidates, yet they would not baptize them. An elder present at the meeting thought that these gospel friends still needed to understand the truth, so he started to speak from the Bible and then from the hymns. When I saw the situation, I became more clear within. I knew that the more he talked, the more he would surely hinder people from being baptized; people might repent and believe, but they would not be baptized. Therefore, I waited for an opportunity.

After the elder finished his talk, the host also spoke something; then there was a "selah." If everyone had been like Job speaking eloquently with long discourses, I would have had no way, but when the "selah" came, this gave me a good opportunity. Immediately I turned to the most promising gospel friend and asked him if he had prayed before. He said that he had not. Therefore, I turned to Romans 10:13 and showed him the verse, which says, "Whoever calls upon the name of the Lord shall be saved." Then I led him in prayer and finally asked him to pray by himself. After that, I asked him what Romans 10:13 says. He answered, "Whoever calls upon the name of the Lord shall be saved." I asked him if he had called upon the name of the Lord. He said that he had. I asked him if he was saved. He answered that he was saved. Then I led everyone to congratulate him for his salvation. Next I asked him to read the first half of Mark 16:16, which says, "He who believes and is baptized shall be saved." As he was going to continue reading the second half, I said, "No need to read on; that part is for those who will perish. You only need to read this part of the sentence: 'He who believes and is baptized shall be saved.'" I asked him to repeat this sentence a few times, then I asked the host to prepare water for baptism. He was baptized within fifteen minutes. An elderly sister even went and got a camera to take pictures.

As the baptism was going on, the sister of the host's daughter-in-law came with a sister in the Lord; this one was also a very good "gospel contact," for she was also not yet baptized. I was very clear within that this one also should be baptized. Right after the brother was baptized and had his picture taken, this new sister was also baptized. This would have been impossible in a big meeting. At the end the elderly sister said, "Brother Lee, for thirty years I had not spoken with you. Today I am very happy that I can have my picture taken together with you." How do you feel about this kind of meeting? If someone comes to visit the church in Taipei and sees this kind of home meeting with speedy baptisms and also with picture taking, he might ask, "What kind of meeting is this?"

Matters That Require Our Study

For this reason we need to have more research. I do not have time to visit all the serving saints in Taipei. If I would visit them, I believe that they would have excellent ideas. Some might just smile, while others might be sad and shed tears. Some of the elders may feel that the church has been supplying several full-timers every month, and even though they heard that several hundreds were baptized and many homes were opened, they could not see any increase in the number of people in the meeting hall. They "heard the thunder but saw no rain." So where are the people? This may be compared to someone who hears that people planted fruit trees in the orchard and that the trees have grown very well and have borne much fruit, but he is not able to taste any of the fruit. What is this all about? On the one hand, the baptismal pool in hall number three is not idle throughout the day. In one moment someone on the street was brought in by the full-timers to be baptized; in another moment a taxi driver who was saved when the saints rode in his cab and preached the gospel to him was brought in to be baptized. This surely is very encouraging. On the other hand, the situation of the meetings also makes one sad. For this reason, we need to have some study and adjustment.

In our training, on the one hand, we are researching and experimenting, and on the other hand, we are also correcting. Therefore, we need subjective experiences. Because of my work in translating the Recovery Version of the New Testament, I do not have much time to research; you are my best assistants here. I would very much like to know what your feelings are concerning the practice of the new way since you have been going out every week to preach the gospel by door-knocking and to hold meetings in the homes. After all, is the practice of the new way proper? Is it convenient? Is it economical? Is there any room for improvement? I need your study and help in all these matters.

Firstly, the greatest matter that we need to study is the result of our knocking on doors for visiting people. Up to the present we have already visited close to twenty thousand homes with seven hundred and ten persons baptized and more than eighteen hundred homes welcoming us to revisit them. But have you considered how we are going to follow up and take care of them? Concerning the eighteen hundred homes, if we need to visit them once a week, how are we going to do it? And who can go? Secondly, now we have no problem bringing people to salvation; we can get a person baptized with only fifteen minutes of gospel preaching. But to be baptized is not to graduate and obtain a ticket to heaven. The recently baptized ones are like newborn babies. After we have begotten them, we should not neglect them; if we do not nourish or cherish them, they will surely die prematurely. To have remaining fruit depends on how we nourish and cherish them as a nursing mother. If we do not do well in this matter, then the churches will rise up to condemn us, saying that people were baptized too hastily and therefore have become premature babies, and that since we baptize people before the time is ripe, so many of them die after baptism. Therefore, this is also a big problem that requires us to carefully study and make improvement. Thirdly, concerning the new believers, how should we bring them to the church? Once a person is saved, spontaneously he is in the church and becomes a member of the church. But how do we bring them practically into the church life? This matter also needs to be studied.

BEING AN EXPERIMENT AND NOT A DECISION

In addition, I would like to make a serious statement: What we are studying and practicing here is not to be made public yet. Even when the saints in your locality ask what kind of training you are having and what we are teaching you, you have to explain it politely, without publicizing. We are not strictly prohibiting you to speak about what we are doing here. But what we are practicing and studying here is mostly experimental; hence, before we have some definite steps in a procedure, I want only you trainees to know, and it is best that the others do not know. This is not because we are trying to keep a secret here, nor is it because we are doing some hidden, shameful things. But before we have results from our research, I do not wish for everyone to be spreading rumors. What we are doing today might be changed tomorrow; if it is being spread outside from one to the other, this will cause many difficulties. I hope that we are clear on this point.

I also know the love of the saints. Although they are not in the training, they want to know what we are doing here and how we are leading here that they may closely follow. But we have also learned from previous mistakes. We did this in the past, but eventually the result was not good and even not sweet. This time the Lord has led us to have a new beginning, but nothing has been finalized; therefore, it is not time to put it forth yet. I told the saints in the United States, "We will let you know what we are doing and practicing. Whatever we do not let you know, you do not need to know. When we succeed in our research and have found by experimenting the concrete, workable steps, then we will teach you the whole thing and tell you how to do them. You will not miss anything." Therefore, before we have the confidence, we should not make it known.

For this reason I am crying out in desperation here, hoping that those in the United States, Canada, and even the whole world can hear my cry: I urge all of you not to be anxious because now we are still in the stage of research; after the results of the research come out, you all can enjoy with us. However, human beings are human beings; hence, they are still very anxious and they insistently question what we are doing here. Now there are saints from the United States and Canada who desire to come and join the training; many who are not accepted feel very sad within, and they long to find out what is going on.

Recently, the brothers from Tainan came to make a request. More than ten saints serving full-time in their locality were not accepted into the training because they did not have sufficient education. When the training is going on here, they are very burning within; therefore, they requested that they be allowed to watch the video tapes of the training. I said that we are not afraid for the content of the training to be known, so there is no harm to let them watch the video. But after watching they must not go and carry it out right away, because they will surely not be able to practice it properly. To sum up, do not be anxious about what to do; nothing good can come out of hastiness. When it is necessary to slow down, we need to slow down.

Take for example the translation of the Recovery Version of the New Testament. This burden is very heavy, but it cannot be rushed at all. When we first started, it was I who was encouraging the translators from behind. Now that we have come to the book of Romans, they turned around and said that it will not be too hard. When I heard this, I only said that now we are just starting to climb a high mountain; I did not want to say that now we are just beginning to be crucified. The grammar in Paul's Epistles is harder than the grammar in the four Gospels and in Acts; it is not easy to

THE PRACTICE OF THE NEW WAY

produce a translation that corresponds with the original language and at the same time reads like a Chinese composition. For example, we repeatedly considered and studied before we finally decided on how to translate the phrase "separated unto the gospel of God" in Romans 1:1. Another example is the rendering of the phrase "on behalf of His name" in verse 5. In the original language, the preposition used here denotes "for," "on behalf of," "instead of," "in the interest of." It is not so easy to decide which of these four denotations to take. In the book of Romans, every word involves the truth. It is hard to decide on the meaning of even just this one particular preposition. I still have three months here, and I do not have much confidence that I will be able to finish this work. Therefore, we must be quick in doing things but not be hasty. We cannot do anything well by being hasty.

I am very fast in doing things, but when it is necessary to be slow, I am very slow, because a fine and delicate work must be done slowly. For instance, about half a year ago I announced that I would put out the Gospel of Matthew as a sample, but until now it is not yet out. This is due to the inclusion of "The Chart of the Seventy Weeks and the Coming of Christ, with the Rapture of the Saints" in the Gospel of Matthew as an appendix. I had intended to draw the chart here in the spring, but I was limited by time, energy, and manpower, thus I did not start. Then I went back to the United States to hold the summer training there, and after its conclusion, I began to draw the chart. Then during my rest on the mountain I continued to draw until I came back to Taipei. During this period of time I made many long distance telephone calls, making corrections repeatedly. What I mean is this: In order to have a good product, I do not wish to do a rough job; rather, I want to do a fine job.

Let us use this training as a further example. three days ago your trainer told me that when you went out to knock on doors, you did not do it one hundred percent according to the way established by the training; instead, you did it mostly according to your natural way. This morning he told me that now more than ninety percent of the time, you do it according to the new way. According to my observation, however, perhaps seventy percent of what you are doing is according to the way established by the training, and the remaining thirty percent is by trusting in your own natural way. I have the confidence to say that the way established by the training came out of our repeated research, so you must follow it. It is the same in doing anything, not only in this matter of door-knocking. We can take calligraphy as an example. If you want to write nicely, you need to copy or imitate by using a copy-book, tracing each stroke accurately; you must not be a bit careless. I myself suffered a great loss in this matter because I did not spend enough effort on it. Therefore, it makes a very great difference whether or not you learn and practice accord-ing to the prescribed way.

This term of training is very special. There is not much homework; it mainly leads you to read the reference books. I wish to make you understand that this term of training does not emphasize the study of the lessons; rather, it emphasizes the practice and exercise. Visiting people by door-knocking is a course of great learning for changing the system to practice the new way. How to take care of the new ones after the door-knocking is an even greater subject of learning, and it is even harder to bring the new ones into the Body life and into the truth. These matters all require our study in many aspects and in a thorough manner. Not only so, I also hope that the Lord's recovery in the days to come will have only one move; I do not wish to create two moves. This is why I do not want our move and our practice here to be publicized, because we are still in the stage of study. If others try to follow what we are doing and if later we make some improve-ments, then they will have wasted their time, and it will also not be easy for them to change. This is like publishing books; if the first edition contains some mistakes, we can put out a second edition with corrections. But the errors in the first edition can never be removed completely because they have already gone out. Therefore, before our research here reaches a final result, I do not want the news to leak out and let others follow what we are doing. Otherwise, if we need to make any correction here, they might not be able to change right away. Consequently, this may affect the future move of the Lord's recovery on earth. Therefore, this matter cannot be rushed at all.

According to the plan, you are going into the villages in January of next year. However, if this new way is not thoroughly studied this year, then next year we will still need to continue to study it, and the plan to go into the villages will have to be postponed. Therefore, everything depends on the result of our study. If our study is not concluded by the time the semester ends, I am afraid that we still will have to come back next year to continue our study together. Maybe some of you can no longer wait; you think that you have already been trained for two years and must now graduate. But I hope that no one is impatient, and everyone will stay on to research together and go on step by step. In summary, what we are practicing is a brand new way, so we must not decide anything in haste. Even the training here is experimental; we are experimenting as to how to conduct the training. Besides Brother Watchman Nee, none of us has done this before. You have to be clear on this point.

I believe that you have received a certain amount of training and have seen some of the things here; therefore, you are eager to bring these things to practice in the churches. But you have to receive my word here: Do not be anxious to do anything. Even when people ask you, you have to answer, "I am not clear what the brothers will do." By all means do not publicize.

CONTINUING OUR STUDY AND IMPROVEMENT

From now on, once every week we will have a study of the new way for its improvement. I hope that in every session of study we can draw a conclusion according to which you can all go and experiment again. Then perhaps the results achieved will be manifested. The main points of our study will be: Are the methods of the new way convenient? Are they economical in time, in energy, and in monetary expenditures?

According to my observations, at present we can draw several conclusions. First, although the time of our research has not been very long, visiting by door-knocking has definitely been proven to be an effective way. Second, if we want to proceed in the new way, the primary thing we need to learn is to deal with ourselves seriously that our inner condition may be proper. For example, do you have enough prayer? Are your sins completely dealt with? Do you have the infilling of the Holy Spirit? Is your spirit uplifted and released when you go out? All the other outward conditions are secondary, and they can be taken care of gradually. The first thing is that your person must be right. This means that your prayer must be sufficient and thorough, your sins must be dealt with thoroughly and completely, and your spirit has to be filled and saturated by the Holy Spirit so that your inner being is completely open, released, rich, and overflowing. Once this kind of spirit comes out, it can produce all kinds of effects; when it touches people, it can cause them to be open and released.

Third, when you visit people by door-knocking, do not think that it will be smooth and easy. On the contrary, you have to realize that there surely will be some difficulties. Someone said that he knocked on thirty to forty doors and none of them opened, so immediately he was disheartened. But I would say that you should not be discouraged because according to our reports, on the average only one in fifty doors we knock on opens up. Someone who researched business advertising said that if there is a two-percent response from the advertisements mailed out, the expenses will be recovered, and if there is a three-percent response, then there will be a profit. I also did a little research the door-knocking by the Mormons and the Jehovah Witnesses and found out that they get one open door only after knocking on hundreds and thousands of doors. Therefore, when you go door-knocking, you must have a proper attitude: An unopened door is not discouraging but rather a normal thing. You must be prepared that people are not going to open their doors. If everyone would open the door and were all predestinated by God, then would it be necessary for us to labor in this matter? I believe that God did not predestinate that many people. However, we also should not say that since God has not predestinated so many, we do not have to labor so much. This is not right. Whether or not God has predestinated a certain one, we do not know, but we must go and knock on the doors to visit people so that those who have been predestinated by God can be found. Therefore, do not be distracted by the fact that people do not open their doors.

Fourth, door-knocking requires certain skills. We need to know what to say when we meet someone and how to converse with him. We must study and learn this. The most important point is that you must avoid aimless speaking and learn to cope with all kinds of situations by remaining calm. Whether or not you are welcomed, you must always find a way to "promote your sales." If someone would not open the door to invite you in but would speak to you only at the door, then you should take the opportunity to show him *The Mystery of Human Life*. Perhaps in one minute you will be able to gain him. Someone may say that he does not have time or that he believes in another religion, but do not pay attention to his excuse. You simply must try to seize an opportunity to show him your "merchandise."

Fifth, according to Acts 1:8, the principle of door-knocking is to go from close by to far away; we must not give up the nearby ones for the faraway ones. As you are serving in the various meeting halls, you should first knock on all the doors in the neighborhood of the meeting hall. If you have a good plan, you will save effort and expense.

Sixth, you must always remember that your work must not be affected by the results. When the result is good, of course you can be happy, but do not be too happy. When the result is bad, you must not be affected and become discouraged. When you go to work, you definitely must have a goal, that is, to bring the Triune God to people, to bring the new believers into the church life, and to perfect them to get into the truth. You must have an accurate view of this goal and hold on to it firmly.

FOLLOWING THE TRAINING'S PRESCRIBED RULES, NOT DEPENDING ON THE NATURAL WAYS

You all can testify that the most effective way for door-knocking is to follow the way established by the training. The other ways, the natural ways, may appear to be helpful superficially, but in fact they are damaging to you. For example, when my child was learning to play the piano, I saw the teacher strictly charge her, saying, "You must not play with your fingers according to your convenience. You must play the way I tell you to play. You may feel that it is very effective to play according to your convenience. Eventually, you will discover that it is very damaging to you." In the same manner, you may feel that to speak with people according to the way established by the training is very foolish and also ineffective, but in reality its effectiveness is invisible to you.

When you go door-knocking, if there are local saints coordinating with you, of course it is a very big help, but you must not rely on them. I hope that you may become experts in the matter of door-knocking. Therefore, in the training you must surely practice strictly, absolutely following the way established by the training. You are allowed to be flexible and make some changes in the details, but you must surely keep the principles.

A WORD OF CHARGE

I also remind you that in door-knocking, the situation of some of the homes may be not good today, tomorrow, or the day after tomorrow, but perhaps on the fourth day it will be good. Therefore, if they do not reject you absolutely, you may go back to visit them. However, it takes manpower to do this. Therefore, I already told the elders that I hope they can bring at least one-fourth of the saints to coordinate together, not to knock on doors every day but to do it at least once a week. At present, Taipei has four thousand saints who meet regularly. If one thousand of these saints can go out once a week and knock on at least five doors, then in a month we can knock on and visit twenty thousand homes. The result will be tremendous.

What we are studying here is a long-term, realistic, and serious practice. We do not want merely a momentary practice out of our enthusiasm. Therefore, I hope that everyone will take this matter seriously and do careful research. For example, in playing basketball, as long as someone can dribble, he can play the game and pass the ball around. But if someone wants to play basketball for the long-term and play it effectively, then he must practice seriously according to the instructions of the coach. If, instead of diligently practicing the basic movements, a person cares only for his own convenience, then it may be profitable in the short term, but in the long run it will be of no benefit and will even be harmful. At present when you go out, you are still practicing; in a year or two you should be able to be coaches when you go back. However, you must not be proud to consider yourself an expert and demand that everyone listen to you. When you have finished this training, I will also instruct you on how to face the elders and how to deal with the older saints when you go back so that the churches may go on in one accord.

What you need to learn now with all your effort is to practice and practice again in the training. Those who learn to play the piano told me that they take only one lesson a week, but they have to practice several hours every day. This is what you should do. If you spend a lot of effort to practice diligently every day in confessing your sins, asking to be filled, releasing your spirit, being uplifted in spirit, and going out every day, then you will spontaneously grow in life. Furthermore, you will become proficient through your constant practice. The tone, the gesture, the speed, and the rhythm of your speaking will all be proper. In this way people will naturally want to open the door to hear you speak.

Therefore, I hope that you will do your best to spend time practicing. You may have to give up some of the meetings in the meeting halls. This is because what we hope is not that you assist the meetings in the various meeting halls; rather, we hope that your time will be spent on practicing. When your practice results in proficiency, you will be a tremendous help to the meeting halls or churches when you go back. Therefore, do your very best to practice, and write a report on the results so that we may study them together and make improvements and then continue to practice. In this way the Lord surely will give us a beautiful perspective.

CHAPTER TEN

AN EVALUATION OF
THE PRACTICE OF THE NEW WAY

(2)

In this chapter, first we will speak about research and then about improvement. In your most recent going out to visit people by door-knocking, you baptized more than one hundred persons, and some of the teams even baptized more than ten. This rate is amazing, and it proves that you have become very proficient through practice. This reminds me of the time when I first came to Taiwan. Taiwan did not produce pears and grapes, so the Americans came to help by forming the Agricultural Restoration Committee solely for the purpose of researching the cultivation and improvement of the various kinds of fruit trees. Their practice was to first find the good seeds and then find the most suitable way to grow them. Consequently, today Taiwan produces delicious pears and grapes. This shows us that regardless of what we do, we need to research and improve.

GOOD SEEDS

Now no doubt in the Lord's recovery we have the best "seeds," *The Mystery of Human Life* being one of them. It is likely that we still can produce even better booklets. This requires our research and improvement.

Seventy years ago when I was just beginning to learn things, due to the high infant mortality rate, the average life expectancy of the Chinese was only about fifty. Now the average life expectancy of the Chinese is over seventy; the reason is that the child mortality rate now is very low due to the advancement in medicine and diet. Although the United States is rich, the people there are negligent in the matter of diet; it is as if they are committing a slow suicide. I am not a physician, but I was sick with tuberculosis forty years ago and spent two and a half years recuperating before I completely recovered. Hence, I also learned some medical knowledge. Actually, there are three things that the Americans should not consume. The first thing is tobacco. Even the United States government requires tobacco companies to place a label on cigarette cartons warning that "smoking may cause cancer." Now it further requires that the label be changed to say that "smoking will cause cancer." The Americans, however, are not afraid to die, and a great number of them are still smoking.

The second thing that people should not consume is cured pork; this is according to the research of the United States government. Twenty years ago, the medical profession, based on the autopsy of soldiers killed in the Vietnam war, discovered that many of these young soldiers had about two-thirds of their blood vessels blocked. This indicates that the majority of young Americans have this condition. Accordingly, we may infer that they may die before the age of fifty due to blockage of the blood flow. The third thing is desserts. Young people in America may listen to their parents when they are still very young, but as they grow up, they do not eat a good breakfast but rather eat doughnuts and other sweet things. The more they eat sweets, the sooner they die. These are statistics from the medical field which we cannot help but believe.

In the Lord's recovery, our seeds are all good; we have neither "cured pork" nor "desserts." In 1954 I had a summer training in Hong Kong, and I told the saints clearly that there is nothing in Christianity today. When you go to the Christian bookstores, you cannot buy any "food"; even if there is some "food," it is just "small candies." But the truths which I have received from the Lord and the messages which I have released do not contain any "sugar"; they are like authentic Shangtung steamed bread. When the southerners make steamed bread, they always add sugar to it. But the really tasty steamed bread does not need anything added to it; it is made in such a way that the fragrance of the wheat comes out. Today's so-called Peking cuisine, which previously was the imperial cuisine, is actually the Shangtung cuisine, which is the highest art of cooking in China. The reason that the Shangtung cuisine is so good is that it does not have added ingredients; rather, it brings out the original flavor of the things created by God. Like the Shangtung cuisine, the messages I give are of the real natural flavor, without other things added and without eloquence. I simply serve the original flavor of the revelations given to me by the Lord.

Why is your visitation by door-knocking so speedy and effective? It is because the materials we gave you are good seeds. To use *The Mystery of Human Life* as the seed is right, but I hope that we can still improve it. I would like to see *The Mystery of Human Life* enriched with a small amount of "protein" and "aged ginseng." Protein is very nutritious and can make one restful; the "aged ginseng" can strengthen and sustain one's life. I have been told that when someone is about to die, if he eats a slice of aged ginseng, he will be sustained for five days; hence, it is precious. If *The Mystery of Human Life* contains these two ingredients, then your door-knocking surely will be even more effective.

GOOD TECHNIQUES

Not only should we have the right seeds, but we should also have the right techniques. When we visit people by door-knocking, we should not say too much, nor should we speak our own words. We should just bring out our "merchandise." When we speak to people, we must seize the opportunity to show them the treasure. Like those who sell diamonds or jade, we simply show people our merchandise. We deal with them as our "target" and try to "sell" them our treasures.

But we must improve the techniques we use. When you knock on a door and realize that the husband and wife in that home have just finished quarreling and are still angry, then you must quickly depart because you perceive that the atmosphere is not right. If you try to sell your goods, I am afraid that not only will they refuse to listen, but they will even vent their anger on you. When you encounter this kind of situation, do not waste your time. Instead, just say that you will come back another time and then quickly depart to knock on another door. You are sent to gain the "sons of peace." If you knock on eighteen doors a day, three or five of those who open the doors may be sons of peace. If they are not sons of peace, do not waste your energy. This is something that you must remember.

STUDYING THE GOD-ORDAINED WAY
FOR THE INCREASE AND SPREAD OF THE CHURCH

The recent reports I received greatly encouraged me. Some teams went out and immediately had eight to ten baptisms; obviously the result has increased. But after we have improved our techniques, there is still the need to promote this matter to the whole church. Formerly, we could not get people saved very quickly. We had to bring them to gospel meetings again and again, and then we had to visit and teach them before we could give them an interview for baptism. If they did not pass the baptismal interview, they had to come back again. Sometimes it took two to three months to lead someone to salvation. Now it takes only fifteen minutes to lead a person to be saved and baptized. In general, the saints may have some doubt, but doubting is unnecessary. We must get rid of this kind of prejudice and continue to improve our techniques. We can use transportation as an illustration. Fifty years ago it took forty-eight hours by boat to go from Chefoo to Shanghai. Now it takes only twelve hours to go from California to Taiwan. In the same principle, previously we often used the love feast as a way of preaching the gospel, but now the method has advanced and improved. It is true that the saints fervently loved the Lord and they also loved human souls, but they did not have the right way to love, so they wasted their time, money, and energy. Now, because we have discovered a more economical way, we hope to save everyone from further suffering. However, the saints need our help because it is not easy for them to change their concept.

Many of you can testify that when you coordinated with the local saints to visit people by door-knocking, at the beginning they were not convinced at all. They considered that they had twenty or thirty years' experience of preaching the gospel and that you were just saved not long ago, so they wondered how much you could possibly know. Eventually, your way is effective and you can get people saved immediately. Even though the saints know a great deal, their result is not as good as yours. In the last elders' meeting, one of the elders testified that he brought several saints with him and went out in coordination with the full-timers to knock on doors to visit people. He preached the gospel to an old man, but after he talked for a long time, the old gentleman still was not saved. Then a full-time sister said, "Don't talk anymore. Let us speak about baptism now." At that moment the wife of the older man came in, and the elder told the full-time sister to preach the gospel to the old woman, and he himself continued to talk to the old man. Not long afterward the old woman wanted to be baptized, so the sister asked the elder to baptize the woman, while she herself continued to speak to the old man. After the old woman was baptized, the old man also wanted to be baptized. When the elder saw this, he could not help but be convinced.

THE GOD-ORDAINED WAY
BEING THE MOST EXCELLENT WAY

My intention in speaking to you repeatedly about all these things is to change your concept. I feel that you are still neither pure nor poor within. In particular, most of the brothers who are over thirty years old still trust in their old natural ways. This training has clearly taught you not to speak many words and not even to take out the booklets, but just focus on the person and subdue him with one sentence. I believe that you young sisters have the faith. The brothers have a "big head," so most of them waver between doubt and belief and still prefer to speak more. Actually, to speak more or to speak less is not the important point; what is important is whether or not we touch the person. This is the same as the principle of blessing others.

If our preaching the gospel by door-knocking can be as effective and as rich in content as injecting someone with a vaccine, then we can consider this step a success. Recently a brother testified that while he was riding in a taxicab, the driver told him that he had just been saved and that now he cannot drive recklessly as he did before because he felt God was forbidding him within. This proves that our injection is working in him. It is useless to merely teach people. Our way is to inject Christ into people as their life supply. Then spontaneously there will be a reaction in them.

Therefore, our training here is a research. We are studying how to improve the product, how to strengthen the word used for injection, and also how to improve our techniques. I believe that you all can confirm that the way given to you in this training is a refined and excellent way; furthermore, it is being continually improved. Please recall that at the beginning of this training, when you first went out to knock on doors to visit people, the result was not good, because you were not yet skillful. Now you have become experienced and the result is manifested. Therefore, what you need is to be poor in spirit and pure in heart and go out to knock on doors according to the instructions you have received in the training. This will bring in the best result.

THE PERSON NEEDING TO BE RIGHT

Of course, both the seeds and the techniques are important, but the person is even more important. The seeds have to be right, the techniques have to be right, and even the more we the laboring ones have to be right. Do you pray enough? Is your confession of sins thorough? Is your fellowship with the Lord transparent? Are you strong in your spirit? These matters will all affect the result of your labor. The seed is the same and the technique is also the same, but the laboring of one who is right will yield a richer harvest, while the laboring of one who is not right will not get good results. We also need to study the matter of how to be a right person. However, at most this training can give you only some basic instructions. What you need most is to continually practice on your own until you yourselves feel that you are right. The seeds in the Lord's recovery are right and the techniques the training gives you are also right, but if your person is not right, then it is not workable. We must have the right seeds, the right techniques, and the right persons.

THREE BURDENS

Up to the present moment, we have already knocked on more than thirty-eight thousand homes, of which more than twelve hundred homes opened their doors while the others either did not open or had no one at home. There were one thousand and thirty-four persons who were baptized and 2,397 homes that want to be visited again. These ratios are quite high; they exceed the ten percent that I expected. But there are three matters that require our careful study. These are also three burdens that I wish to mention.

1. Taking the Family as a Unit

First, we need to make a slight change of direction in our practice; that is, instead of paying attention to individuals, we should focus on the entire family. This means that in our gospel preaching we must take the family as a unit. To do this, the best way is to gain the parents first. If the parents are not saved yet and the children are still in the custody of the parents, then when you baptize the children, problems may occur and lead to the parents' opposition. But if you lead the parents to salvation first, then it is easier to gain the next generation. Therefore, we have to study how to lead the parents to baptism first and then gain the entire family.

Of course, you should not do this in a rigid way. Sometimes when you visit a home, the parents avoid you. Then you should not refrain from preaching the gospel to the children just because the parents avoid you. However, we hope to work on the parents first; then it will be easier to lead the children afterward. We want to avoid problems that may arise by neglecting the parents and working on the children first. We have to study this point carefully so that we may avoid this kind of problem.

2. Being Economical in Time

Second, in the training we also want to study how to help you manage your time. In other words, we need to study how much time you should spend from now on when you go to visit and take care of the baptized saints. After you lead someone to be saved and baptized, it may be all right if you do not revisit him in a week, but it is not so good if you do not visit him again for two weeks, and you may lose him if you do not revisit him for three weeks. Not only so, you still have to set aside a part of your time to continue knocking on new doors. You may not be able to knock on as many doors as before, but you must not stop altogether. Therefore, now we have to study how, after baptizing people, we should use our time to continue visiting them and establishing meetings in their homes and how we should allocate our time for revisiting and for knocking on new doors. This needs much research.

3. How to Conduct Home Meetings

After a person is baptized, we still need to continue to revisit, to take care of him, and to establish a meeting in his home. But what should we do in this meeting? And how should we do it? This matter requires our study in depth. After we have led a person to salvation, we must then lead him to grow in life. To lead someone to grow in life, we cannot stay away from the truth; without the truth it is very difficult for him to grow. Therefore, you need to probe for a way to teach the truth to lead people to grow in life. Of course, in the Lord's recovery there is a great deal of material on the truth. However, we need to draw up a plan concerning which materials to use and how to compile them properly. This may be likened to holding the rudder steady when sailing the boat; otherwise, the boat cannot proceed in a straight course and time will be wasted.

When you lead others to grow in life and to get into the truth, eventually you will be able to lead them into the church life. When people are saved and baptized, immediately they are in the church, but they are not living in the church life yet. Our basic goal is to bring them into the church life. I am not referring to bringing them to our big meetings. Our big meetings at present are a mixture of the old and the new; they are just like the water at the mouth of the Yangtze River which is partly salty and partly fresh. I am concerned that if the newly saved ones come to the big meetings and see the old situation, a situation of the so-called worship, they may receive some bad influence. Therefore, I would rather not have them attend the big meetings temporarily so that not only will they avoid the bad influence, but they will also receive a good impression of the church life in the homes. However, this is not an easy thing to do.

THE PRESENT DEFINITE PRACTICE

There are less than three months left in this term of training. I hope that you can thoroughly research these points and carefully experiment with them; thus, when you go back to the locality you came from, you may be able to present the results of the training and what you have learned here. Prior to that time, I do not wish to let the churches in the various localities know too much because of the fact that our present practice is not so accurate yet. If they should know about what we are doing here and immediately try to do the same thing and they do not get the ripe fruit, then that will not be so good. Hence, this matter cannot be rushed. It is not until this training has researched enough and has practiced thoroughly that we can present all these things to all the saints. Then you all can be teachers and coaches. In other words, I hope that this training can be like a teachers' college that specializes in producing teachers and coaches to promote the practice of the Lord's new way.

Concerning the practice of the new way, at present we already have some very definite steps. The first step is to knock on doors and to baptize people. There are some distinctions between door-knocking and visitation. The goal of door-knocking is to preach the gospel to people, leading them to be saved and baptized, while visitation is to visit and take care of those who have already been saved and baptized. These ones are not only familiar to us, but they have also become our kinsfolk, our brothers and sisters, in the Lord. Hence, when we go, it is to visit them. Therefore, door-knocking is to contact new ones, the unsaved ones, for the preaching of the gospel, while visitation is to revisit someone who has already been saved and baptized.

The second step is to visit the newly baptized ones and establish a meeting in their homes. In the home meetings we need to do the following three things: First, we need to help people get into life and grow in life; second, we need to help them get into the truth for their advancement in life; and third, we need to carry out our basic goal, which is to lead them into the church life. Primarily and for most of the time, this church life should take place in the homes.

STEPS STILL BEING RESEARCHED

The third step, which is still being experimented on, is to set up the small group meetings. After you have baptized a person and have continued to visit and take care of him three to five times, you must fellowship with him about gathering the new ones in his neighborhood and taking turns having small group meetings in each other's homes. In this way you will not only economize the time in visiting and taking care of them, but you will also be able to perfect them together corporately. Especially in helping them to know the truth, if you are speaking to just one or two persons, the taste will not be so rich. But if three or five families can come together, with perhaps eight or ten persons there, the taste will be much richer when you teach them the truth. At the same time you can teach them how to meet by singing, praying, reading the Scriptures, and testifying.

At present we already have good seeds and good techniques for the preaching of the gospel by door-knocking to lead people to salvation. However, concerning how to lead them to grow in life, learn the truth properly, and enter into the church life, we still need to find the "good seeds." We do not need to write new teaching materials; we just need to find the suitable materials from the existing publications, and with a little amount of editing we can compile them into messages for edification, such as how to pray, how to read the Bible, and how to offer money or material things.

SOME DETAILS THAT REQUIRE OUR ATTENTION

Concerning door-knocking and visitation, you must draw up a plan in principle. You must clearly plan from now on how much time you will spend on door-knocking to preach the gospel and how much time to visit those who have already been baptized. On the other hand, due to the different situations of the different districts, you cannot be too rigid and inflexible. You need to observe the local situation and the conditions of the people and earnestly look to the Lord in prayer for His leading concerning the allocation of your time. If you make decisions without allowing any room for minor modifications, that will annul the Lord's leading.

Since one of the goals of this training is to evangelize the whole island of Taiwan, in the future you will all be going to the villages. Then you may have to speak Taiwanese instead of Mandarin. For this reason, if you meet some native Taiwanese during your door-knocking and visitations, it is best if you practice speaking in Taiwanese. Those of you who do not speak Taiwanese must try your best to learn to speak it, and during the door-knocking and visitation, you should let those who can speak Taiwanese demonstrate it first.

Another point to which you must pay attention in door-knocking is that you must not do it only once. I already said that in some of the homes there may not be sons of peace today but tomorrow there may be some. Furthermore, in some of the homes which you knock on today, only the children are home and the parents are not there, or nobody may be home. You need to keep a record, with remarks concerning all these situations, and find time to knock on these doors again. You need some practice in this matter.

According to my personal observations and considerations, after leading a person to salvation, we must consider the care for the new one as our primary responsibility; otherwise, all our previous efforts will be nullified. We may not be able to spend all of our time on this aspect, but this must have the priority. This matter requires your careful study and practice to find out its relative weight.

We also have to pay attention to another matter, that is, the newly saved ones always have some questions about ordinary matters such as the worship of ancestors and the eating of the foods offered to idols, and also some questions about particular matters such as Catholicism and Mormonism. We have to write several kinds of booklets, so that when asked by someone about any of these questions, we can give him a booklet to solve his problem.

All the things mentioned above not only should become the rules of our practical training, but in the future they will also be passed on to all the churches. We may not be able to thoroughly research all of these points during this term, but they must be the goals toward which we strive. I hope that you may all see this matter clearly.

THE SPIRIT AND THE BURDEN OF THE NEW WAY

We have to see clearly the goal of the new way. The failure of Christianity is due to the forsaking of the homes and relying on big meetings. This is the biggest reason for the failure in Christianity. We must take the way of recovery by leaving the big meetings and coming back to the homes. The results of the new way will be gospel preaching in the homes, leading people to grow in life in the homes, leading people to know the truth in the homes, and having the church life in the homes. The home, not the individual, is the unit.

Let me use the Chinese people as an illustration. About a hundred years ago, China was technologically underdeveloped and remained in a very conservative condition, so Japan went ahead of us. Then, being ambitious to conquer China, Japan used all its efforts to invade China. Although the Chinese have a bad character in being indecisive and sloppy, they responded all over the country to resist the Japanese, and the whole nation entered into the conflict. I saw with my own eyes that when the Chinese government sent out a call, all the people rose up by families and the whole nation went into resistance. They came from everywhere, from the east, the west, the south, and the north, and they included everyone, the young, the old, the males, and the females. Consequently, Japan had no way. By sending two to three million strong soldiers to China, they thought that in a year or two they could conquer China, but in the end they surrendered in defeat. From 1895 to 1945, after fifty years of war, the Chinese eventually won the war. The reason for the victory was the Chinese family. The Chinese culture and the foundation of China as a country are built upon the family. Neither the Mongols nor the Manchus were successful in conquering China; in the end they were all assimilated and blended with the Han people. The reason still lies with the family. For thousands of years the Chinese family has been the base upon which the country was built. Regardless of the change of governments, no one can defeat the family.

I give you this illustration so that you may see that the failure of Christianity is due to their having only big meetings and thus not having a foundation. Moreover, what they do is one-sided. The triumph of the Chinese culture lies with the family. Therefore, you all have to see clearly that the Lord's way among us today is to build up all the spiritual things, including the truth, life, and the church, in the homes. When the homes rise up to function, the result will be tremendous.

When I was young, transportation in China was not convenient; there was quite a distance from the north to the south. When I began to work for the Lord, I was sent out to many places from the north to the south. I observed that although in China the dialects were different in various places, the culture was the same. The ethical and moral culture of China was passed down from generation to generation and was established in the homes. This resulted in the preservation of the Chinese culture, which is the foundation of China. Therefore, today we also want to adopt this way, that is, the building up of all the spiritual things in the homes. Only this will be powerful, universal, and far-reaching. Consider this: If we can raise up ten thousand homes in Taipei, that would be a tremendous matter; if we can raise up thirty thousand homes in Taiwan, then Taiwan will really be evangelized. Therefore, this is worthy of our research and practice.

Having meetings is like going to classes; if you do not go to school, you do not learn anything. But if you attend a poor school, then the English you learn there will have the wrong pronunciation and the wrong grammar. As a result, it may be helpful temporarily, but eventually it is harmful for you. The big meeting is not a "good school." The things taught there may help people temporarily, but ultimately they will hurt them. However, because we are in the stage of changing the system, we cannot "quarantine" the big meetings immediately; rather, we will still use them temporarily as a substitute in consideration of the situation. However, I would rather that you use all your effort toward working on the homes, bringing all the people and all the matters into the homes. I hope that you all may strive and seize the time to practice and to study well, thereby paving the new way that the Lord's recovery may proceed on a great highway!

ABOUT THE AUTHOR

Witness Lee was born in 1905 in northern China and raised in a Christian family. At age 19 he was fully captured for Christ and immediately consecrated himself to preach the gospel for the rest of his life. Early in his service, he met Watchman Nee, a renowned preacher, teacher, and writer. Witness Lee labored together with Watchman Nee under his direction. In 1934 Watchman Nee entrusted Witness Lee with the responsibility for his publication operation, called the Shanghai Gospel Bookroom.

Prior to the Communist takeover in 1949, Witness Lee was sent by Watchman Nee and his other co-workers to Taiwan to ensure that the things delivered to them by the Lord would not be lost. Watchman Nee instructed Witness Lee to continue the former's publishing operation abroad as the Taiwan Gospel Bookroom, which has been publicly recognized as the publisher of Watchman Nee's works outside China. Witness Lee's work in Taiwan manifested the Lord's abundant blessing. From a mere 350 believers, newly fled from the mainland, the churches in Taiwan grew to 20,000 in five years.

In 1962 Witness Lee felt led of the Lord to come to the United States, and he began to minister in Los Angeles. During his 35 years of service in the U.S., he ministered in weekly meetings and weekend conferences, delivering several thousand spoken messages. Much of his speaking has since been published as over 400 titles. Many of these have been translated into over fourteen languages. He gave his last public conference in February 1997 at the age of 91.

He leaves behind a prolific presentation of the truth in the Bible. His major work, *Life-study of the Bible,* comprises over 25,000 pages of commentary on every book of the Bible from the perspective of the believers' enjoyment and experience of God's divine life in Christ through the Holy Spirit. Witness Lee was the chief editor of a new translation of the New Testament into Chinese called the Recovery Version and directed the translation of the same into English. The Recovery Version also appears in a number of other languages. He provided an extensive body of footnotes, outlines, and spiritual cross references. A radio broadcast of his messages can be heard on Christian radio stations in the United States. In 1965 Witness Lee founded Living Stream Ministry, a non-profit corporation, located in Anaheim, California, which officially presents his and Watchman Nee's ministry.

Witness Lee's ministry emphasizes the experience of Christ as life and the practical oneness of the believers as the Body of Christ. Stressing the importance of attending to both these matters, he led the churches under his care to grow in Christian life and function. He was unbending in his conviction that God's goal is not narrow sectarianism but the Body of Christ. In time, believers began to meet simply as the church in their localities in response to this conviction. In recent years a number of new churches have been raised up in Russia and in many eastern European countries.

OTHER BOOKS PUBLISHED BY
Living Stream Ministry

Titles by Witness Lee:

Abraham—Called by God	978-0-7363-0359-0
The Experience of Life	978-0-87083-417-2
The Knowledge of Life	978-0-87083-419-6
The Tree of Life	978-0-87083-300-7
The Economy of God	978-0-87083-415-8
The Divine Economy	978-0-87083-268-0
God's New Testament Economy	978-0-87083-199-7
The World Situation and God's Move	978-0-87083-092-1
Christ vs. Religion	978-0-87083-010-5
The All-inclusive Christ	978-0-87083-020-4
Gospel Outlines	978-0-87083-039-6
Character	978-0-87083-322-9
The Secret of Experiencing Christ	978-0-87083-227-7
The Life and Way for the Practice of the Church Life	978-0-87083-785-2
The Basic Revelation in the Holy Scriptures	978-0-87083-105-8
The Crucial Revelation of Life in the Scriptures	978-0-87083-372-4
The Spirit with Our Spirit	978-0-87083-798-2
Christ as the Reality	978-0-87083-047-1
The Central Line of the Divine Revelation	978-0-87083-960-3
The Full Knowledge of the Word of God	978-0-87083-289-5
Watchman Nee—A Seer of the Divine Revelation ...	978-0-87083-625-1

Titles by Watchman Nee:

How to Study the Bible	978-0-7363-0407-8
God's Overcomers	978-0-7363-0433-7
The New Covenant	978-0-7363-0088-9
The Spiritual Man • 3 volumes	978-0-7363-0269-2
Authority and Submission	978-0-7363-0185-5
The Overcoming Life	978-1-57593-817-2
The Glorious Church	978-0-87083-745-6
The Prayer Ministry of the Church	978-0-87083-860-6
The Breaking of the Outer Man and the Release ...	978-1-57593-955-1
The Mystery of Christ	978-1-57593-954-4
The God of Abraham, Isaac, and Jacob	978-0-87083-932-0
The Song of Songs	978-0-87083-872-9
The Gospel of God • 2 volumes	978-1-57593-953-7
The Normal Christian Church Life	978-0-87083-027-3
The Character of the Lord's Worker	978-1-57593-322-1
The Normal Christian Faith	978-0-87083-748-7
Watchman Nee's Testimony	978-0-87083-051-8

Available at
Christian bookstores, or contact Living Stream Ministry
2431 W. La Palma Ave. • Anaheim, CA 92801
1-800-549-5164 • www.livingstream.com

Comment ne pas concevoir une plante plus propice à la poésie que la « plante sensible » ? Aussi connue sous le nom de plante timide ou encore *touch me not*, elle possède des feuilles se rétractant au toucher, se ferme complètement dans le noir et s'ouvre à la lumière.

Poésie en Fleurs a été réalisée par Riviere & Son à l'aide d'un vert marocain. La pièce centrale est la plante sensible, entourée de chambres dans lesquelles apparaissent des flocons ainsi que différents feuillages, fleurs et papillons riches en couleur et en contraste. La reliure originale fut utilisée pour le recueil de P.B. Shelley, *The Sensitive Plant and Early Poems*, lequel emploie la plante sensible comme un emblème pour explorer les façons de trouver de la signification et de l'ordre dans un monde allant de plus en plus vers l'entropie et le chaos. Notre couverture représente une célébration des humeurs de l'esprit créatif. Nous espérons que les utilisateurs de nos carnets Poésie en Fleurs seront inspirés par le style contemporain choisi pour cette collection.

Es gibt kaum eine poetischere Pflanze als die durchaus passend bezeichnete „schamhafte Sinnpflanze". Das auch Mimose genannte Gewächs hat empfindliche Blätter, die sich bei Berührung schnell zurückziehen. Auch in der Dunkelheit schließen sich die Blätter und öffnen sich bei Licht.

Das auf unserem Einband Blühende Poesie reproduzierte Muster stammt von den Buchbindern Riviere and Son und bestand aus grünem Marokkoleder mit Goldverzierungen. Das Mittelstück zeigt eine Mimose und ist umringt von Feldern mit Schneeglöckchen sowie anderen farbenfrohen Blumen, Blättern und Schmetterlingen. Die Originalbindung enthielt das Werk (*The Sensitive Plant and Early Poems*) des Dichters Percy Bysshe Shelley, in dem die schamhafte Sinnpflanze ein Symbol für die Suche nach Sinn und Ordnung in einer Welt ist, die zu Entropie und Chaos neigt.

Unser Einband ist eine Hommage an die vielfältigen Stimmen des kreativen Geistes. Wir hoffen, auch du lässt dich vom zeitgenössischen Stil der Bindung dieser Notizbuchs inspirieren.

È difficile immaginare una pianta più propizia alla poesia di una il cui nome è "pianta sensitiva". La pianta sensitiva (*mimosa pudica*) è dotata di foglie che si richiudono al tatto. Si chiude al buio e si apre alla luce.

Il disegno riprodotto sulla copertina di Poesia in Fiore è stato realizzato da Riviere and Son in marocchino verde con filature dorate al suo interno. L'elemento centrale è una pianta sensitiva, circondata da sezioni decorate con bucaneve e altri fiori, foglie e farfalle dalle tonalità ricche e contrastanti. La rilegatura originale è stata utilizzata per *La pianta sensitiva e primi poemi* di Percy Bysshe Shelley, dove l'autore impiega la pianta sensitiva come emblema per esplorare la ricerca del senso e dell'ordine in un mondo che tende all'entropia e al caos.

La nostra copertina è una celebrazione dei numerosi stati d'animo non solo dello spirito creativo. Speriamo che lo stile contemporaneo della rilegatura che abbiamo scelto per questo diario possa ispirarti.

Pocas plantas tienen un nombre tan poético como la llamada «mimosa sensitiva». Esta planta, también conocida como vergonzosa, planta de la vergüenza o nometoques, se repliega al mínimo toque de sus hojas. Además se cierra por completo en la oscuridad y se abre con la luz.

El diseño que reproducimos en nuestra cubierta Poesía en Flor fue confeccionado por Riviere and Son en marroquín verde con filetes dorados. El motivo central es una mimosa sensitiva, rodeada de campanillas de invierno y otras flores, plantas y mariposas de tonos vivos. La encuadernación original corresponde a la obra *The Sensitive Plant and Early Poems* de Percy Bysshe Shelley, que emplea la mimosa sensitiva como símbolo para intentar encontrar orden y significado en un mundo que tiende al desorden y al caos.

Esta cubierta celebra las numerosas facetas del espíritu creativo. Esperamos que el estilo contemporáneo de encuadernación que hemos elegido para este diario le sirva de inspiración.

含羞草(はにかみそう)、これほど詩的な植物がほかにあるでしょうか。葉に触れるとたちまち小さく縮んでしまうことからこの名がつきました。別名「オジギソウ」、または「ネムリグサ」(英語名「sensitive plant」)とも呼ばれ、暗くなると葉が閉じ、光が当たると開くという特性を持っています。

このシリーズは、緑のモロッコ革に金箔装飾を施した Riviere and Son 製の装丁を再現したものです。中央の含羞草をぐるりと囲む形で、スノードロップをはじめ、色鮮やかな花々、植物、蝶の図柄が配されています。原版はパーシー・ビッシュ・シェリーの「はにかみ草および初期詩編」で使用されたものであり、無秩序と混沌のなかで意味と秩序を見出す術を探ることの象徴として、含羞草が用いられています。

豊かな創造性を存分に感じられ、コンテンポラリーなスタイルを採用したデザインが、使う人の感性を刺激するものであることを願ってやみません。

paperblanks®
POETRY IN BLOOM

Poetry in Bloom

One can hardly conceive of a plant more conducive to poetry than the aptly named "sensitive plant." The sensitive plant (*mimosa pudica*), also known as the shy plant and touch-me-not, has leaves that shrink away from the touch. It closes tight in the dark and opens to the light.

The design reproduced on our Poetry in Bloom cover was crafted by Riviere and Son and made with green morocco within fillets of gilt. The centrepiece is a sensitive plant surrounded by chambers containing snowdrops and other richly hued and contrasting flowers, foliage and butterflies. The original binding was used for *The Sensitive Plant and Early Poems* by Percy Bysshe Shelley, which employs the sensitive plant as an emblem for exploring how to find meaning and order in a world that leans toward entropy and chaos.

Our cover is a celebration of the many moods of the creative spirit. We hope that you will be inspired by the contemporary style of binding we've chosen for this journal.

ISBN: 978-1-4397-5358-3
ULTRA FORMAT   176 PAGES   LINED
DESIGNED IN CANADA